JEWS and CHRISTIANS After the HOLOCAUST

JEWS and CHRISTIANS After the HOLOCAUST

ABRAHAM J. PECK, Editor

Foreword by ELIE WIESEL

FORTRESS PRESS Philadelphia

Library of Congress Cataloging in Publication Data
Main entry under title:

Jews and Christians after the Holocaust.

Essays read at a symposium sponsored by the Hebrew Union College-Jewish Institute of Religion, in Cincinnati.
Includes bibliographical references.
Contents: Introduction : religion in a post-Holocaust world / Alfred Gottschalk—Defining the Holocaust / Yaffa Eliach—Christology and Jewish-Christian relations / Rosemary Radford Ruether—[etc.]
1. Christianity and other religions—Judaism—1945– —Congresses.   2. Judaism—Relations—Christianity— 1945– —Congresses.   3. Holocaust, Jewish (1939–1945) —Influence—Congresses.   4. Christianity—20th century— Congresses.   5. Judaism—20th century—Congresses. I. Peck, Abraham J.   II. Hebrew Union College-Jewish Institute of Religion.
BM535.J47   209'.04   81–70665
ISBN 0–8006–0678–7   AACR2

9397K81   Printed in the United States of America   1–678

To my parents, Shalom and Anna Peck,
who have bequeathed to me the survivors'
legacy of humanism,
and to my wife, Jean,
and children, Abby and Joel,
for understanding that legacy

Contents

Foreword

Dear Abraham Peck:

Thank you for allowing me to read and study these essays. I regret not having heard them. Fred Gottschalk describes with great feeling the mood of the conference room: You should all be congratulated. There exists no subject capable of dividing—or of galvanizing or bringing together—people, such as the one which you and your colleagues have attempted to explore at your colloquium. I hope your meetings have brought you closer to one another—and to our dead whose history influences and will continue to influence ours for centuries and centuries to come.

In truth, friend, I admire all those—philosophers, poets, theologians, essayists, and psychologists—who take part in all those gatherings devoted to the "Kingdom of Night." I confess, not without embarrassment, that I myself rarely participate in them. Surely I would like to understand, but I know I never shall. Even when I have read all the documents, gathered all the testimony, heard all the judgments, all the ideas, and all the theories, I still will not understand. And so I am afraid.

I am afraid of attending debates where, unwillingly or even unwittingly, someone will make use of the events out of their context, of phrases whose meaning has disappeared with those who disappeared, of words which belong to another world, to a vanished universe.

I myself am stumbling on increasingly real obstacles: I can no longer articulate certain images, certain expressions. For example, I no longer can refer to the Holocaust. A term that no longer evokes the fear and the mystery of the beginning. It is being used and abused here and there with and without reason: It no longer burns the lips that utter it.

Lately, I am experiencing difficulties speaking about this subject; the abyss between the survivor-witness and the others is becoming deeper and deeper. The more—and the more carefully—people listen to us, the more we realize that our words are not "getting through"; what we try to say is not what you think you have heard.

Is it because the theme has been too commercialized in too many domains? These days, one says "Auschwitz" and goes on speaking of other things; or one makes a passing remark about "Treblinka" and continues doing other things. There was a time when we used to tremble—literally—before uttering those names. Nowadays, one sees them again and again—in magazines, on TV, at the theater, or at the movies: It seems they have even made a musical comedy of it somewhere.

And yet, and yet. Is silence a solution? If it simply replaces the spoken word, the answer is no. If it penetrates the word so as to sear it, to endow it with its necessary tragic dimension, the answer is yes.

Thus, we are trapped. We must speak, write, teach, analyze, educate, compare documents and testimonies; we must serve as living, integral links between the dead and future generations—so as to save the ones from forgetfulness and the others from death.

Therefore, these meetings of men and women from diverse backgrounds, expressing themselves in the name of various traditions, seem fruitful to me, and even essential. What they have said here has often touched me. Am I to express my friendship with one speaker or my disagreement with another? As a general rule, I feel close to the one who asks the questions, and surely closer than to the one who insists on giving answers.

For the believer, no question can cause such anguish, such anxiety, and—why not say it?—such despair. God and Birkenau do not go together. How can you reconcile the Creator with the destruction by fire of one million Jewish children? I have read the answers, the hypotheses, I have reread the theological solutions offered: The question remains question. As for answers, there are none; there ought to be none.

In the *Black Book*, the anthology of Ilya Ehrenbourg and Vassily Grossmann about the destruction of Russian Jews during the Occupation, you can read the story of a Jewish mother somewhere in the Ukraine whose two children were decapitated before her eyes. Seized by madness, she grasped the two mutilated corpses and began to dance. She danced and danced while the killers watched her and laughed. Finally, they killed her, also.

This woman dancing with her dead children keeps me from sleeping. I tell myself that she is trying to communicate something to us by her dance, and from beyond her madness, and I ask myself what that could be. And—strange—I know this is linked to the conflicts haunting me concerning faith, language, the humanity of mankind, and the compassion of heaven.

A story in the same anthology portrays a Jewish coachman, Hayim-Aron, who has miraculously escaped the massacre. But he refuses to be the only survivor of his community. So he starts running towards the synagogue, grabs hold of a *Sefer-Torah*, and arrives exhausted at the very spot where the killers are killing his neighbors, his friends, his parents. He asks to be allowed to hold the Torah while he is being killed, so as not to die alone.

Here again, I fail to understand what this simple coachman is trying to teach me. But I realize that it has to do with a hard and implacable truth, profoundly human and perhaps eternal. Will I know it someday? I am afraid to say yes, and I am afraid to think no.

I have told you: This subject fills me with fear. Always. With uneasiness too, I admit. I wish I had found, in these pages, in your discussions, a bit more love for the Jewish victim, a bit more understanding toward their survivors in Israel—therefore, toward Israel— and a bit more humility toward the specific and quasi-ontological aspect of a Jewish tragedy, the greatest of Jewish tragedies, equal to no other, a tragedy whose implications are universal. Remove then, the anti-Semitic element—the Final Solution invented for the Jews exclusively—and the Event would lose its mystery. I have said it elsewhere: Not all the victims were Jews, but all Jews were victims.

Having said all this, it is my duty to add: I believe this Event ought to bring us closer now rather than separate us. Thanks to this Event, the world may be saved, just as because of it, the world is in danger of being destroyed.

ELIE WIESEL

Preface

Writing in April 1946 in the *Landsberger Lager Ceitung*, one of the earliest and best of the Jewish DP camp newspapers, J. Nemenczyk related a concentration-camp fantasy which he had experienced lying in lice-filled straw, in hunger and in pain. "I had a vision," he wrote, "that if the world could not give us back our dead brothers and sisters, then it could give us back a moral world."[1]

Little could Nemenczyk know, either in the concentration camp or in 1946, that the concept of a "moral world," for which he so longed, had been murdered in the same spot as his dead brothers and sisters.

The absence of a moral world was not the only bitter disappointment that Holocaust survivors faced in the years immediately following liberation. Professor Elie Wiesel, the voice and the soul of survivors in America, expresses another side to this disappointment: "After liberation . . . as they [the survivors] reentered the world, they found themselves in another kind of exile, another kind of prison. People welcomed them with tears and sobs, then turned away." The survivors were "disturbing misfits who deserved charity, but nothing else." What they wanted, according to Wiesel, was to "transmit a message to you, a message of which they were the sole bearer. Having gained an insight into man that will remain forever unequaled, they tried to share their knowledge with you, their contemporaries. But you discarded their testimony."[2]

I know the sense of that disappointment and bitterness only too well. My parents are survivors of the Holocaust, survivors of the Lodz Ghetto, of Auschwitz, of Buchenwald, of Stutthof, and of Theresienstadt. I also know something about the "insight" mentioned by Wiesel, and about the resulting survivor ideology, which sought and failed to change the direction of Jewish destiny and of human destiny, to steer a course toward the moral and social perfection of humanity.[3]

It was thus with a special sensitivity and with a special commitment that I accepted the invitation of Professor Alfred Gottschalk,
president of the Hebrew Union College-Jewish Institute of Religion, to plan and organize a symposium called "Religion in a
Post-Holocaust World." The symposium was held at the Hebrew
Union College-Jewish Institute of Religion in Cincinnati on November 19 and 20, 1980. Over twelve hundred people attended the
various sessions, including seminarians and their professors from
over a dozen Catholic and Protestant seminaries in Ohio, Indiana,
and Kentucky. This particular aspect of our symposium led to two
evenings of intense dialogue, perhaps for the first time in history,
between male and female students of Christian and Jewish
seminaries.

It is hard to put into words what the symposium meant for me
as a scholar, as a Jew, and as a child of Holocaust survivors. Perhaps, as with some aspects of the Holocaust, it is best to remain
silent, where words will not suffice. But for others, words came
quickly. For many Christian and Jewish seminarians it was "the
most moving and educational experience of my seminary career."
For others in our audience it was a revelation, the opportunity to
take back with them a terrible new knowledge. As Franklin Littell
has stated, the story of the Holocaust and its consequences allows
the listener an immediate confrontation: "Either you get it or you
don't. Once you get it nothing will ever be the same again."[4] This
was the goal of our symposium, and it is the hope of the Hebrew
Union College-Jewish Institute of Religion that nothing will ever be
the same again for those who participated in our symposium, for
those who saw a national television news program devoted to the
events of the symposium, and for those reading this volume.

The essays included in *Jews and Christians After the Holocaust*
were read at the major sessions of the symposium. They have been
revised and edited for publication. The essays attempt, as a whole,
to evaluate the place of religious values in a world which has been
forever changed by the events commonly referred to as the Holocaust. These events are well-known. Between the years 1939 and
1945, six million European Jews were destroyed as part of a
genocidal scheme formulated by Nazi Germany, a scheme which

had as its final solution "the destruction of the entire Jewish people." Beyond this horror, at least five million non-Jews perished, the victims of political and other related murders. These are figures which the civilized human mind can barely comprehend. Yet the ultimate lessons of the Holocaust do not lie in statistics.

Indeed, the essays in this volume concern themselves with what one American Christian theologian has called "the death-knell for at least a certain kind of Western civilization,"[5] the most telling consequence of the Holocaust. This death knell, the authors believe, discredited many of our accepted values—religious, secular, and intellectual. The essays challenge the complacency of Christians and Jews in accepting the Holocaust without giving thought to the fact that it may only have been a foreshadowing of what is yet to be.

The challenge in this book is to both Christians and Jews—the challenge to prove that their faiths, values, and moral systems are essential and still operative in the world after the Holocaust. These essays ask whether our contemporary religious faith and beliefs, unchanged as they seem to be despite assertions of historical Christian theological anti-Judaism and of international Jewish failure to rescue during the Holocaust, can preserve for us the shared hopes of Christians and Jews for a future of global community and peace. In light of continuing brutalities by individuals against individuals and nations against nations, does the Holocaust mark the decline of our Western culture and its systems of moral thought and beliefs? Can our religious institutions in fact shape human behavior and society to a future state of redemption that transcends both Christians and Jews?

It is now my pleasure to thank publicly a number of individuals and institutions whose many efforts helped to bring about this volume. I am grateful to Dr. Samuel Greengus, Professor Lowell McCoy, Jessica Baron, Adrienne Polster, and Tidg Faust, all of whom are now or were with the Hebrew Union College-Jewish Institute of Religion. I am further grateful to Dr. Richard Jameson, the Reverend Monsignor Lawrence K. Breslin, and Charles Tobias, active participants in the many interreligious affairs of Cincinnati. I am very grateful to a dear friend and significant contributor to the dynamics of our symposium, Dr. Carl Hermann Voss. I must also thank the Ohio Program in the Humanities and its executive director, Dr. Charles Cole, as well as the Greater Cincinnati Foundation and its director, Jacob Davis, for financial assistance which made the November 1980 symposium possible.

I am further grateful to the fine senior representatives of Fortress Press, Norman Hjelm and Dr. John Hollar, for believing in the importance of our symposium papers and to my editor, Edward Cooperrider, for his editorial assistance. Finally, I must thank Professor Alfred Gottschalk, president of Hebrew Union College-Jewish Institute of Religion, for his guidance, his support, and his belief in the legacy of the Holocaust survivors and in the enormous value of Christian-Jewish dialogue.

ABRAHAM J. PECK

Hebrew Union College-Jewish Institute of Religion
Cincinnati, Ohio
September 1981

Notes

1. J. Nemenczyk, *Landsberger Lager Ceitung,* 15 April 1946, p. 3.
2. Elie Wiesel, *A Jew Today* (New York, 1978), pp. 185–208.
3. On the development of this ideology see Abraham J. Peck, "An Introduction to the Social History of the Jewish DP Camps: The Lost Legacy of the She'erith Hapletah," in *Proceedings of the Eighth World Congress of Jewish Studies* (forthcoming). A Hebrew-language version will appear in 1982 in the journal *Gesher* (Jerusalem).
4. Franklin Littell, "Lessons of the Holocaust and Church Struggle: 1970–1980," summarized in *Journal of Ecumenical Studies* (Spring 1981): 371.
5. Eva Fleischner, in *Auschwitz: Beginning of a New Era?* ed. idem (New York, 1977), p. x.

Introduction:
Religion in a
Post-Holocaust World

ALFRED GOTTSCHALK

During two unforgettable days in November 1980, over a thousand Jews and Christians were witness to a series of lectures and discussions which questioned the very authenticity of their religious beliefs. The symposium, entitled "Religion in a Post-Holocaust World," was presented by the Hebrew Union College-Jewish Institute of Religion in Cincinnati.

I will return to this in further detail a bit later. I think it is important that I now set out some of our reasons for presenting such a program. Between 1935 and 1942, the Hebrew Union College was instrumental in bringing out of Nazi Germany nearly a dozen Jewish scholars—scholars whose academic qualifications often had little or nothing to do with our own teaching needs—and enough students from Germany so that by 1938 these German Jewish refugees made up 12 percent of the total enrollment of our student body.[1] I do not think that during the years up to 1942 we knew any more than the rest of the American Jewish community that our actions would precede the destruction of European Jewish life. But perhaps the world-famous Talmudic scholar Michael Guttmann, head of the Budapest Rabbinic Seminary and father of Alexander Guttmann, one of the scholars we brought over who is still teaching here today, knew better: "What the College is doing," he wrote to us during those years, "is a deed which has its unique historical value and will remain memorable for all times. It is a noble rescue, not alone of the Jewish teacher, but also of Jewish teaching."[2]

1

Whether we could have done more—both as a rabbinical seminary and as a community—is one of those questions which are now a part of historical controversy. Yet Hebrew Union College, to its credit, grasped the significance of the European Holocaust months after the end of World War II. In 1947 my predecessor, Dr. Nelson Glueck, authorized the founding of the American Jewish Archives, an internationally respected institution whose major aim was and still is to aid American Jews in facing the awesome responsibility of preserving the continuity of Jewish life and learning. In that same year the Christian Fellows Program was initiated at Hebrew Union College. The aim of this unique interfaith effort—which has awarded more than two hundred fellowships and granted over fifty Ph.D.'s to Christian scholars—can best be summarized in these words:

> When these ministers have completed their studies at the College and have gone out into their practical ministry or into the academic world of their own divinity schools, our hope is that they will teach the Christians of America that which the rabbinical students must teach the Jews of America and what we must all teach one another —namely, that the human heart is big enough to embrace all men and that the divine spirit is within us all.[3]

It was only natural then that during those two momentous days we asked Christians and Jews alike to ponder with us whether our contemporary religious faith and beliefs could preserve for us the shared hopes of Christians and Jews for a future of global brotherhood and peace.

I

Writing in 1945, Dwight MacDonald reflected on the events in Europe from 1933 to 1945. "Something has happened to Europe," he wrote. "What is it? Who or what is responsible? What does it mean about our civilization, our whole system of values?"[4] For MacDonald, indeed for the major portion of American and European liberal thinkers, a great catastrophe had taken place. Their world view of rationality and steady progress toward international peace had been smashed to pieces, victim of the "belief that humanity had set limits to the degradation and persecution of one's fellow man."[5] In a similar vein, the historian Henry L. Feingold has stated that the nations of the West "were unable to fathom that Auschwitz meant more than the mass destruction of European Jewry." He has observed that "it perverted the values at the heart of our civilization." Even today, he argues, "few thinkers have made the link between the demoralization and loss of confidence in the West and the chimneys of the death camps. . . . Today as yesterday, few understand that a new order of events occurred in Auschwitz, and that our lives can never be the same again."[6] I cannot help thinking of the anguish of the Viennese Jewish writer Stefan Zweig, writing about the new order of things as a refugee from Nazism in Brazil. "We of the new generation," Zweig wrote, in opposition to "that idealistically blinded generation [prior to World War I] . . . have learned not to be surprised by any outbreak of bestiality; we who each new day expect things worse than the day before, are markedly more skeptical about a possible moral improvement of mankind."[7] Zweig's skepticism drove him and his wife into suicide a few short months later.

The symposium "Religion in a Post-Holocaust World" addressed itself to the "new order of events" brought about by the chimneys of Auschwitz. Yet those events may be hard for us to grasp. In fact, some authors have expressed the view that the Holocaust "will never be assimilated in terms of the familiar normative thought structures provided by Western history and culture."[8] After all, the Holocaust was not and is not an historical crisis in the normal sense. The Holocaust was not a revolution: there were no great changes in ideas of political and governmental power; it was not an economic collapse (the economic system was hardly influenced); nor were there great boundary changes, or new and great reforms of religion or views of human nature, or scientific impact. It is rather in the breakdown of morality that the crisis can be understood best, in the corruption of all standards of ethics and value judgments and in the clear understanding that "neither traditional law nor religion could prevent . . . the massive killings."[9]

We are faced today with the recognition that the Holocaust was a revaluation of all moral values—a clear sign that Western civilization had failed, that the illusion of order, of progress, of religious tolerance and understanding, the cornerstone of that civilization, was merely that—an illusion. If millions of innocent people could be systematically destroyed at the center of European civilization, then that civilization was entirely incapable of providing moral security to its inhabitants. Since the Holocaust was possible, we must understand that prior religious and cultural values were susceptible to corruption, that those values were impotent in the face of the Holocaust.

The Holocaust has made it clear that neither of the two pillars of Western morality—religion and law—was adequate in protecting human beings; that in fact Western religious institutions have never been able to stand up to the power of the modern state. Is there any evidence to suggest that religious institutions have any greater ability to influence national policies today than they had in Hitler's Germany?

One can clearly see this dilemma in the plight of the Christian churches in Germany. Outside of a very few clergy and lay persons such as Probst Heinrich Gruber, Gertrud Luckner—both honored by the Hebrew Union College-Jewish Institute of Religion—Father Lichtenberg, and Hans and Sophie Scholl, among others, very few of Germany's Christians were able to overcome the inherent tension "between individual action and the demands of abstractions linked to the State, the Church and history."[10] This tension was most prevalent in the peculiar phenomenon of the public-private split in German religious life that began with Martin Luther.[11] Even the writings of Dietrich Bonhoeffer during the early Nazi period reflect this. Bonhoeffer wrote in 1933:

> Without doubt the Jewish question is one of the historical problems which our State must deal with, and without doubt the State is justified in adopting new methods here. . . . The Church cannot in the first place exert direct political action, for the Church does not pretend to have any knowledge of the necessary course of history. Thus even today, in the Jewish question, it cannot address the State directly and demand of it some definite action of a different nature. . . . It is not the Church but the State which makes and changes the law.[12]

By the end of that year and thereafter, Bonhoeffer had overcome this historical tension and strongly deplored the Nazi policies against the Jews—and one must hold him in the highest regard for his letters and papers from prison, where he argued for a "this-world and a non-religious Christianity."[13] Yet more the norm was the case of the *Deutsche Christen* (the "German Christians") and the *Deutsche Volkskirche* (the "German people's church") which was founded by Dr. Artur Dinter and based upon the myth of race and soil. Dinter was the same man who two decades earlier had written a novel entitled *Sin Against the Blood,* which for the first time in Germany advanced racist ideas in the context of a novel.[14]

Yet I do not wish to single out Germany in the collapse of our Western religious values. I do not even wish to focus on the Second World War; a close reading of history will show that the collapse and the revaluation of values had its beginnings in the First World War and that many of the actions taken by the Nazis, including the unparalleled lack of fear of world opinion in carrying out the "final solution," stem from the 1914–18 period. Witness the pronouncement by the racist Pan-German Heinrich Class on the Jews in October of 1918 to "kill them all. The rest of the world, in judging these actions, will not ask for your reasons."[15]

I would tend to agree with Arnold Toynbee, who observed that "a Western nation [like Germany], which, for good or evil, had played so central a part in Western civilization . . . could hardly have committed these flagrant crimes if the same criminality had not been festering below the surfaces of life in the Western world's non-German provinces."[16]

II

One scholar, in pondering the events of the Holocaust, has written: "What remains is a central, deadening sense of despair over the human species. Where can one find an affirmative meaning in life if human beings can do such things!"[16a]

I believe it has been the "troubled conscience" of Christians and also Jews that has sought to come to terms with the meaning of the Holocaust, especially in the last half decade.[17] On the part of the Christian community this has entailed a critical self-examination and scrutiny, examining the Christian tradition for signs of an historical anti-Semitic attitude which seemingly begins with statements by John and Paul, statements such as the one by John that Satan is the father of the Jews and the remark by Paul that Jews were the enemy of humanity.[18] Christian theologians have established a line of continuity in the "teaching of contempt" for the Jews—in the words of Professor Isaac—a line which stretches from John Chrysostom to Martin Luther to Adolph Stoecker to the German Christians. Perhaps Rabbi Richard Rubinstein has correctly summed up this Christian view of Jews as "the best of saints and the worst of sinners but never as a simple human being. . . . There is a polarity of images in Christian thought on Jews and Judaism which extends from Jesus to Judas but knows no middle ground."[19]

The Holocaust too has caused much concern and rethinking in the Jewish community as well, for we are the defendants in the charges by the eminent Holocaust survivor and spokesman—and my dear friend—Elie Wiesel that American Jewish leaders did not do enough to help save European Jewry: "Jewish leaders met, threw up their arms in gestures of helplessness, shed a pious tear or two and went on with their lives . . . as usual." And Wiesel condemns us for neglecting the survivors of the Holocaust: "In the beginning they tried to raise their voices . . . in vain. People turned away and, shrugging their shoulders, muttered 'Poor devils . . . they want our pity.' . . . No; they did not want your pity . . . all they wanted was your attention . . . to transmit a message to you, a message of which they were the sole bearers."[20] What was that message? It was the insight into humanity, as Wiesel puts it, "that will forever remain unequaled."[21]

It is too late for us to listen, I fear. The survivor community, apart from Wiesel's magnificent voice, is entirely too still, and is disappearing through age and illness. They are taking away with them a "legacy that could have changed the world."[22]

It is rather for us to explore the meaning of the Holocaust for Christians and Jews and to rediscover that legacy, focusing upon not merely the sociopolitical problems engendered by the Holocaust—not only the problem of Christian anti-Semitism and what can be done about it—but the problem of evil in general; not only the relationship between Christianity and Judaism, but that between man and God.

Yet I firmly believe that we cannot approach the meaning of the survivors' legacy by attempting to understand what they endured:

> The killers' laughter . . . the distant look of old men who knew
> . . . the screams . . . the moaning . . . the beatings . . . the silent,

almost solemn processions marching toward the mass graves or the flames: the lucidity of some, the delirium of others . . . the little girl undressing her little brother as she tells him gently . . . not to be afraid . . . for one must not be afraid of death; and the woman who on the edge of hysteria begs the killers to spare her three children, and receives this response: Very well, I shall take only two; tell me which two. . . .[23]

I will respect my friend Wiesel's wish for me not to try and understand this experience. During our symposium we did not try to understand what he understands. But we also have to live with the meaning of Auschwitz for our religious beings, and so we must search for the legacy.

In conclusion, I wish to add one more observation. There are many well-meaning Christians among us who so identify with the suffering of European Jewry that they too label themselves as survivors of the Holocaust. They wish fervently to universalize the meaning of this "uniquely unique event," as Alice and Roy Eckardt have termed it,[24] so that its victims may be *the victim*, its lessons *the lesson*, symbols of all human catastrophe and all human suffering. Thus, there are those who, unintentionally, try to enlarge the Holocaust's focus.[25] But the Holocaust was the planned destruction of the entire Jewish people—not all victims of the gruesome death toll during the murderous years from 1933 to 1945 were Jews, but "all Jews," as Wiesel has correctly stated, "were victims." Millions of non-Jews died at the hands of the Nazis, and crimes of national and cultural genocide affecting other nationalities were committed before, during, and after the Holocaust (the ultimate genocide). The Holocaust itself, however, was an event affecting only the Jewish people.[26]

Then why did Christians come to our symposium? For what reasons did they have to be in attendance? Because in Hitler's mad vision of history Christianity, entirely Jewish at its core, was a cancer on the body of the Aryan peoples and thus had to be destroyed along with Jews and Judaism. Dietrich Bonhoeffer knew this over forty years ago. On Crystal Night, November 9 and 10, 1938, as the Jewish synagogues and temples were burning all over Germany, he brushed aside the arguments of theological students who stated that Crystal Night was a fulfillment of the curse on the Jews by answering that "If the synagogues burn today, the churches will be on fire tomorrow."[27]

No, we must not universalize the Holocaust by stating that it proves all things are possible, for we must face the "incredible particularity of the Jewish experience."[28] What then does the uniqueness of the Holocaust mean? Wherein lies its universal meaning? And why were Jews and Christians, over a thousand of them, at our symposium? The black political scientist H. G. Locke has written: "I am forty-four years old. The Holocaust is not my history. My history begins in the black ghetto of Detroit, but the Holocaust is the key event for me as an academic and citizen. Who will be the victims of the future? The passive bystanders? The committers of the deeds? Where do the roads begin today into the next Holocaust?"[29] And what shall we do about it now? This is the challenge before us. This is the challenge of our time.

Notes

1. Michael A. Meyer, "A Centennial History," in *Hebrew Union College-Jewish Institute of Religion at One Hundred Years*, ed. Samuel E. Karff (Cincinnati, 1976), p. 124.

2. Michael Guttmann, as quoted in Michael A. Meyer, "The Refugee Scholars Project of the Hebrew Union College," in *A Bicentennial Festschrift for Jacob Rader Marcus*, ed. Bertram Wallace Korn, (New York, 1976), p. 372.

3. Quoted in "The Christian Fellows Program," publication of the Graduate School, Hebrew Union College-Jewish Institute of Religion, (Cincinnati, n.d.), p. 1.

4. Dwight MacDonald, as quoted in George M. Kren and Leon Rappoport, *The Holocaust and the Crisis of Human Behavior* (New York, 1980), p. 1.

5. Alexander Donat, as quoted in Henry L. Feingold, "Who Shall Bear Guilt for the Holocaust: The Human Dilemma," in *American Jewish History* 68 (March 1979): 281.

6. Ibid., p. 266.

7. Stefan Zweig, *The World of Yesterday* (New York, 1943), p. 4.

8. Kren and Rappoport, *The Holocaust*, p. 12.

9. Ibid., p. 129.

10. Ruth Zerner, "Dietrich Bonhoeffer and the Jews: Thoughts and Actions, 1933–1945," in *Jewish Social Studies* 37 (Summer-Fall 1975): 249.

11. Kren and Rappoport, *The Holocaust*, pp. 23–24.

12. Dietrich Bonhoeffer, as quoted in Zerner, "Dietrich Bonhoeffer and the Jews," p. 240.

13. Ibid, p. 250.

14. George L. Mosse, *Germans and Jews* (New York, 1970), pp. 55ff.

15. Heinrich Class, as quoted in Abraham J. Peck, *Radicals and Reactionaries: The Crisis of Conservatism in Wilhelmine Germany* (Washington, D.C., 1978), p. 235.

16. Arnold Toynbee, as quoted in Eliezer Berkovits, "Rewriting the History of the Holocaust," *Sh'ma* 10/198 (3 October 1980): 141.

16a. Kren and Rappoport, The Holocaust, p. 126.

17. Robert F. Drinan, "The Christian Response to the Holocaust," *The Annals of the American Academy of Political and Social Science* (July 1980): 180.

18. Martin Stöhr, "Holocaust Oder: Konsequenzen Nach Auschwitz," *Judaica* 35/5 (September 1979): 106ff.

19. Richard L. Rubinstein, *After Auschwitz: Radical Theology and Contemporary Judaism* (Indianapolis, 1966), p. 71.

20. Elie Wiesel, *A Jew Today* (New York, 1978), p. 197.

21. Ibid.

22. Elie Wiesel, as quoted in Paula E. Hyman, "New Debate on the Holocaust," *New York Times Sunday Magazine*, 14 September 1980, p. 109.

23. Wiesel, *A Jew Today*, p. 199.

24. Alice L. Eckardt and A. Roy Eckardt, "The Holocaust and the Enigma of Uniqueness: A Philosophical Effort at Practical Clarification," *The Annals of the American Academy of Political and Social Science* (July 1980): 167.

25. A protest against enlarging the focus of the Holocaust can be found in Edward Alexander, "The Incredibility of the Holocaust," in *Proceedings of the Seventh World Congress of Jewish Studies Holocaust Research* (Jerusalem, 1977), p. 94.

26. This point is made quite clearly in two very important works: Yehuda Bauer, *The Holocaust in Historical Perspective* (Seattle, 1978), pp. 30ff., and Uriel Tal, "On the Study of the Holocaust and Genocide," *Yad Vashem Studies* 13 (1979): 7–52.

27. Dietrich Bonhoeffer, as quoted in Zerner, "Dietrich Bonhoeffer and the Jews," p. 246.

28. Alexander, "The Incredibility of the Holocaust," p. 94.

29. H. G. Locke, as quoted in Stöhr, "Holocaust Oder," p. 110.

Defining the Holocaust: Perspectives of a Jewish Historian

YAFFA ELIACH

During the last few years, the Holocaust has become one of the central issues dominating much of our academic, political, social, and cultural activities. It has become a seismograph for measuring and evaluating every minor or major, real or imaginary tremor in Jewish life and the world at large. The Holocaust seems to be a constant evaluative factor whenever we stand on the crossroads of change and decision making. Consciously or subconsciously, the Holocaust is a guiding undercurrent in the interaction between the Jewish people and society, between the world and the Jew, between religion and secularism, between Christianity and Judaism, between human and God, between Jew and Jew. The language and imagery of the concentration camp universe have become part of our daily vocabulary. Holocaust language is used to express the entire range of human experiences, be they brutality, despair, anguish, faith, or freedom. It is sufficient to utter two names, Auschwitz and Anne Frank, and there is no further need to search for synonyms either for the inhumanity of human to human or for humanity's capacity for innocence and hope. Those who cannot cope with the awesome legacy and, above all, the moral implications of the Holocaust simply deny its central issue—the destruction of six million Jews.[1]

We are in a difficult predicament. A simple biological fact, our date of birth, has placed our generation between the society that produced Auschwitz and the one which must come to terms with its legacy. We are a paper bridge on which the weight of a civilization rests. Whatever we preserve from the Holocaust era, endowing the surviving evidence with the respectability of an historical document, will set the criteria for future scholarship. Peter Gay believes that history itself, in an almost implacable Darwinian battle, selects historical data for its permanent record.[2] The modern historian is also an active partner in this process. In our great haste, or perhaps because of the great delay, we select and edit, and at times we omit, misuse, or erase, some essential material of the Holocaust period and its aftermath, thus allowing it to perish. The task is too overwhelming, the material too voluminous, the changes around us too rapid, and the past too vivid. At times we are unable to be objective, or else we are too impersonal and detached.

In both cases we are prisoners of our past and our private or common experience. We use historical data, we use our professional skills and view each other and the world around us through the prism of Auschwitz. Sooner or later, we are bound to issue the verdict of German guilt, of the innocence of the victims and the compliance of the civilian population. A pattern emerges in which World War II society is divided into three major categories: the executioner, the onlooker, and the victim. All of them acted and reacted within the framework of their pasts, carrying their actions and reactions during the Holocaust to their utmost extreme. It is our sordid, almost unmanageable task to document, understand, and analyze the roots of Auschwitz, the cultural Hiroshima of the West. We must transmit our findings to the next generation, which waits in the shadow of the atomic umbrella for our assessments of the Holocaust period. But Holocaust research has recently become not only a probe into a troubled past which leads to an understanding of the evolution of Auschwitz. It has become a huge laboratory of human behavior. It has become a vast scientific experiment where thanks to extant German records of the Holocaust period we can observe human behavior under the most extreme conditions. We conduct our studies into the scarred past from the safe distance of the present. Many of the oppressors, victims, and onlookers are still alive, coping with time, distance, memories, and documents. Some researchers come to the Holocaust "lab" to study human reaction to stress during long endurance of extreme conditions; others, to study the effects of prolonged hunger and starvation on the human mind and body, which were so well documented in the 1942 Warsaw Ghetto study.[3] Still others may be fascinated by medical "ethics"—by the study of the Auschwitz doctors. These men and women who took the Hippocratic oath to save human lives dedicated themselves instead to depriving people of their lives. In these doctors we see the transformation of healers into killers.[4]

In the theater, a fine actress may covet the part of a Holocaust victim not because of her affinity with the subject but because of professional ambitions. The dramatic portrayal of the tormented existence of a concentration camp victim demands of the actress the ultimate range of emotions, intellect, and acting ability. This is a challenge no fine artist can resist. An accomplished novelist may turn to the Holocaust not in order to probe the Auschwitz universe but to use it in order to express other, unrelated ideas more forcefully, to focus on such themes as male-female sexual tensions, the female as the ultimate victim, or even the theme of the artist as a young man. Attaching these literary themes to a Holocaust setting creates the illusion of the ultimate. The Holocaust in such literary works becomes a mere vehicle for the extreme. William Styron's character Sophie Zawistowska, a Polish Catholic survivor of Auschwitz, may be, among others, an example of such usage.[5]

The ultimate in endurance, faith,[6] the will to live,[7] the bestiality of humankind, and the nobility of the human spirit can all be observed in the vast laboratory of the Auschwitz kingdom. The material is easily understood and relatively accessible. It all took place in a society which used the same alphabet we use, the same Roman and Arabic numerals, the same scientific language, logic, ethics, and even religion. The Nazis and their collaborators were Westerners like ourselves.

These unlimited potentialities for using the Holocaust attract to the field of Holocaust studies brilliant individuals from an ever-growing number of disciplines, in an interdisciplinary approach rarely enjoyed by any other subject matter. It is also a double-edged sword. Many studies, some excellent ones, by focusing only on the twelve-year Reich or on particular events during that period tend to overlook the complex interaction of culture, religion, politics, and other factors which conditioned and guided Europe for centuries. We may feel a certain sense of satisfaction in comprehending various extreme conditions that existed during the Holocaust period, but in reality, we may be left only with a manifestation of the effect without searching for the cause. We may miss the strange interplay within the ingathering at Auschwitz of the many aspects of Western civilization.

While examining all the facts, all the figures, all the extreme conditions of the Holocaust period, we may reach a certain numbness. Our sensitivity, sense of moral obligation, and ability for keen historical analysis may be dulled. The reader of Peter Weiss's *The Investigation* is faced at times with a similar reaction. The play is based on transcripts from the Frankfurt trial, on the testimony of Auschwitz camp officials and inmates and on arguments put forward by their counsel. Despite the authentic material, the distinction between the executioners and the victims becomes blurred; they are reduced to faceless, nameless characters. The lines of demarcation between good and evil, humanity and bestiality, guilt and innocence are indistinguishable. Walter Kerr's remarks, a few days after the play opened in New York in November 1966, deserve to be quoted:

> The activity itself is, in the end, without character. It would seem to have nothing to do with life or death, with right or wrong, with love or hate. The brain is its own end, an instrument for doing whatever is to be done as swiftly, as effectively, as intelligently as possible. Literally, mass murder is done intelligently.[8]

It is the responsibility of the historian of modern history to prevent the isolation of Auschwitz from the mainstream of European history, to prevent the study of Auschwitz in an abstract void. It is the task of the historian, philosopher, thinker, theologian, and scholar, Christian and Jew alike, to anchor the Holocaust in European reality and culture.

Conspicuously absent from Holocaust studies in a most visible way is the Jewish historian. Jewish history of the Holocaust period has not yet produced a Raul Hilberg and his extensive research of massive, voluminous German documents of the Holocaust dealing with the destruction of European Jews. It is precisely the state of Eastern European Jewish history in the post-Holocaust era and the nature of Jewish documents from the Holocaust period that are partially responsible for the absence of such a history or an historian. Yet the Jewish historian's role in Holocaust studies should be a central one. Since the victims were all Jews, or, to use Elie Wiesel's phrase, "while not all victims were Jews, *all* Jews were victims,"[9] the insights of the Jewish historian are of paramount importance to the understanding of the Holocaust. The tensions between the history and the origins of anti-Semitism, between Christianity and Judaism, between the emancipated Jew and modernity, especially in Western Europe, have received attention in numerous works, some excellent in their scope and dimension: the studies of Edward Flannery, Rosemary Ruether, Gordon Zahn, John S. Conway, Franklin Littell, Leon Poliakov, Jean-Paul Sartre, Uriel Tal, Hannah Arendt, Jacob Katz, Peter Gay, and George Mosse, to mention a few.

It is rather the Jewish reaction during the Holocaust period as seen by the Jewish historian that scarcely emerges from Holocaust studies. This is crucial to defining and understanding the Holocaust.

One may attribute this lack to the fate of the Jewish historian as well as to the nature and source of Holocaust documents. Many Jewish historians and scholars were themselves victims of the Holocaust. The aging historian and ideologist, Simon Dubnow, (1860–1941), was shot in the streets of Riga. Meir Balaban (1877–1942), considered the founder of historiography of Polish Jewry and its communal institutions, died in the Warsaw Ghetto. Yitzhak Schiper (1884–1943) perished in Majdanek, where he worked in the potato-peeling brigade. Hillel Zeitlin (1871–1942), the Jewish thinker who was preoccupied with the survival of the Jew in a hostile environment, was murdered on the way to Treblinka garbed in a prayer shawl and phylacteries. Yitzhak Katzenelson (1886–1944), whose poem "Song of the Murdered Jewish People" is one of the most tragic Jewish literary documents of the Holocaust, perished in the flames of Auschwitz together with others from the Vittel transport. Emanuel Ringelblum (1900–1944), the chronicler and historian of the Warsaw Ghetto, a member of the Yivo Institute for Jewish Research and founder of the Circle of Young Historians, was murdered on the "Aryan" side of Warsaw after the liquidation of the ghetto.

The deaths of these Jewish historians, and others, the murders of many brilliant Jewish scholars left a void in Jewish scholarship, history, and historiography. European Jews were not only physically destroyed. Their task of documentation was abruptly halted. The natural flow of Jewish scholarship was brutally disrupted. These Eastern European Jewish historians were steeped in Jewish scholarship and its vast spectrum of sources. They were intimately familiar with the millennia-old Jewish social, communal, and religious institutions and the value system that dominated Jewish life in the past. Although many of those same historians were secularists, champions of new political, cultural, and national movements, their prism, regardless of their ideologies, was the rich Jewish heritage. Their murder, during the Holocaust, left a void in Jewish history and thought. With the best intentions and the most outstanding talent, scholars in Israel and the United States, the two emerging centers of Jewish scholarship, cannot instantly fill that gap. In no other area of history is the loss of the Eastern European Jewish historians more keenly felt than in Holocaust studies.[10] A comprehensive knowledge of Jewish history and its cultural values is of paramount importance for the scholar who is investigating any aspect of Jewish reactions during the Holocaust. One may assume that the cultural heritage of the Jewish victim was an important factor in shaping his reactions in the ghetto, camp, hiding place, or partisan movements. It is not sufficient to examine Jewish reaction only against the background of party affiliation, political ideology, and participation or nonparticipation in armed resistance. Each of the above is of cardinal significance; the exclusion of the Jewish factor creates a one-dimensional study of the Holocaust.

Jewish resistance during World War II is one of the best-documented events of the Holocaust, placing it among the major movements of European armed uprisings. It is also of primary importance to examine Jewish resistance within the context of Jewish history and values. Perhaps centuries-old conditioning of collective, communal responsibility and close-knit family ties, among other factors, prevented many Jews from taking drastic action against the Germans and delayed Jewish armed resistance. Armed uprisings were organized in 1943, when most Jewish families were decimated and the final destination of the Jews was clear to some young people, mostly members of Zionist pioneer groups, who by then had nothing to lose but their lives.

> You are asking why the Jews did not resist, why we did not escape to the dense forests, to unite, to gain strength to organize cadres of partisans in order to fight for a better, more beautiful tomorrow?
>
> Two specific factors influenced the multitude of Jews like opium as they permitted themselves to be led to the terrible slaughter without resistance. The first cause was their family ties: the feeling of responsibility toward parents, women, and children. It chained us together with unbreakable bonds and forged us into one inseparable body.[11]

These words were written by Zalman Gradovski, a member of the *Sonderkommando* in Auschwitz. His notes were buried in a trench filled with human ashes.

The last entry in Zalman Gradovski's notes, dated September 6, 1944, reads:

> We, the *Sonderkommando*, have long since wanted to put an end to our terrible work, which we were forced to do under pain of death. We wanted to do a great deed. The camp inmates—some Jews, Russians, and Poles—restrained us with all their might and forced us to postpone the revolt. But the day is near. Our hour may strike today or tomorrow. I write these words at a moment of utmost danger and tension. May the future judge us by what I have written. May the world discern in these jottings the tiniest fragment of the tragic world in which we have lived.[12]

Once the resistance took place in the Warsaw ghetto and in Birkenau by the members of the *Sonderkommando*, was it just a matter of dying with honor, of putting an end to a wretched existence? Or was it the will to live tinged with the old Jewish optimism that David may overcome Goliath and Judah the Maccabee will destroy the Syrian troops and Hellenism? Perhaps there was a chance that the few would vanquish the many after all.

Did Jewish optimism and Messianic yearning delay and hinder Jewish resistance? Did Jews believe that relief was on its way and the Messiah would come momentarily, maybe even at the doors of the gas chamber? While this faith protected the Jew from painful assessment of reality in all its naked brutality, it also lulled so many Jews into passivity.

Many Jewish values during the Holocaust acted as double-edged swords. On one hand they helped to preserve, to some degree, a human self-image in the face of German dehumanization. On the other, they facilitated the speedy, relatively unopposed implementation of the German plans of destruction.

Each major or minor issue involving the Jewish victim during the Holocaust, be it Jewish leadership, the failure to rescue, compliance, physical and spiritual resistance, or any of many other issues, must be examined within the context of the victim's personal and collective national past.

What greatly hinders this approach—studying the victim within the context of his past—is not only the significant absence of the Jewish historian from Holocaust studies but also the nature of a large volume of Holocaust documents. For reasons which are self-explanatory, the number of German documents dating from the Holocaust period greatly overwhelms the number of Jewish documents. Jewish documents from sites of open-air killings and concentration camps are rare. From ghettos, partisans, and hiding places, there is naturally a much larger body of documents. The source and nature of these documents determines the research. When consulting primarily German documents, one can expect a limited view of the subject—that of the executioner and collaborator. A German document[13] listing the murder of 137,346 Lithuanian Jews by Strike Commando 3 and local collaborators between July 4, 1941, and November 25, 1941, is an inventory listing the date, place, and number of murdered Jewish men, women, and children and Communists. The October 27, 1941, entry on Eisysky reads, 989 Jewish men, 1,636 Jewish women, 821 Jewish children; total, 3,446.

Surprisingly, the German document is inaccurate. The massacre in Eisysky took place on the twenty-fifth and twenty-seventh of September. All was quiet in Eisysky on the twenty-seventh of September. As to the number of victims, over four thousand people were murdered, since the toll included the Jews of the neighboring townlets of Olkeniki[14] and Selo. About seven hundred Jews managed to escape to Radin, eight kilometers away. The German document does not even offer a glimpse of the Jews during the last days of their lives. What does it mean when a Jewish community, after eight hundred years of coexistence with its Christian neighbors, comes to such an abrupt, tragic end? How do the Jews face this end? What is the response of their Christian neighbors? Two young men who witnessed the two-day massacre survived. One of them is Zvi Michalovsky.

Jew, Go Back to the Grave

On the eve of Rosh Hashana 1941, all the Jews of the small Lithuanian town of Eisysky were herded together into the two synagogues, without food, water, and toilet facilities. Lunatics from the nearby insane asylum of Selo were appointed as their supervisors. It was clear to the rabbi of Eisysky, Rabbi Shimon Rozowsky, that his beloved *shtetl* was doomed. A few days earlier he had called the town's notables together and told them, "Jews, our end is near. God does not wish our redemption; our fate is sealed and we must accept it. But let us die with honor, let us not walk as sheep to the slaughter. Let us purchase ammunition and fight until our last breath. Let us die like judges in Israel: 'Let me die with the Philistines.' "[15]

Some had supported him, but the opposition, led by Yossel Wildenburg, prevailed.[16] Now it was too late. From the synagogues they were led to the horse market. At the head of the strange procession—more than four thousand Jews—walked Rabbi Shimon Rozowsky, dressed in his Sabbath finery and his tall silk yarmulke. Next to him walked the handsome hazan of Eisysky, Rabbi Tabolsky. The hazan, wrapped in his tallit, was holding the holy Torah scrolls. The rabbi and the hazan together were leading the congregation in the Viddui—confession of the dying.

In groups of two hundred fifty, first the men and then the women, they were taken to the old Jewish cemetery in front of the open ditches. They were ordered to undress and stand at the edge of the open graves. They were shot in the back of the head by Lithuanian guards with the encouragement and help of the local people. The chief executioner was a Lithuanian, Ostrovakas. Dressed in a uniform, a white apron, and gloves, he personally supervised the killing. He reserved for himself the privilege of shooting the town's notables, among them Rabbi Shimon Rozowsky, and he practiced sharp-shooting at the children, aiming as they were thrown into the graves.

Among the Jews in the old Jewish cemetery of Eisysky that September 25, 1941, was one of the *shtetl's melamdim* ("teachers"), Michalowsky, and his youngest son, Zvi, aged sixteen. Father and son were holding hands as they stood naked at the edge of the open pit, trying to comfort each other during their last moments. Young Zvi was counting the bullets and the intervals between one volley of fire and the next. As Ostrovakas and his people were aiming their guns, Zvi fell into the grave a split second before the volley of fire hit him.

He felt the bodies piling up on top of him and covering him. He felt the streams of blood around him and the trembling pile of dying bodies moving beneath him.

It became cold and dark. The shooting died down above him. Zvi made his way from under the bodies, out of the mass grave into the cold, dead night. In the distance, Zvi could hear Ostrovakas and his people singing and drinking, celebrating their great accomplishment. After eight hundred years, on September 26, 1941, Eisysky was Judenfrei.[17]

At the far end of the cemetery, in the direction of the huge church, were a few Christian homes. Zvi knew them all. Naked, covered with blood, Zvi knocked on the first door. The door opened. A peasant was holding a lamp which he had looted earlier in the day from a Jewish home. "Please let me in," Zvi pleaded. The peasant lifted the lamp and examined the boy closely. "Jew! Go back to the grave where you belong!" he shouted at Zvi, and slammed the door in his face. Zvi knocked on other doors, but the response was the same.

Near the forest lived a widow whom Zvi knew too. He decided to knock on her door. The old widow opened the door. She was holding in her hand a small, burning piece of wood. "Let me in!" begged Zvi. "Jew! Go back to the grave at the old cemetery!" She chased Zvi away with the burning piece of wood as if exorcising an evil spirit, a dybbuk.

"I am your Lord, Jesus Christ. I came down from the cross. Look at me—the blood, the pain, the suffering of the innocent. Let me in," said Zvi Michalowsky. The widow crossed herself and fell at his bloodstained feet. "Boze moh, Boze moh,"[18] she kept crossing herself and praying. The door was opened. Zvi walked in. Zvi promised her that he would bless the woman, her children, and her farm, but only if she would keep his visit a secret for three days and three nights and not reveal it to a living soul, not even the priest. She gave Zvi food and clothing and warm water to wash himself. Before leaving the house, he once more reminded her that the Lord's visit must remain a secret, because of his special mission on earth.

Dressed in a farmer's clothing with a supply of food for a few days, Zvi made his way to the nearby forest. Thus, the Jewish partisan movement was born in the vicinity of Eisysky.[19]

The murder of Eisysky's Jews, as stated in the Jewish source, assumes a meaning of a different dimension and magnitude, vital for Christian and Jew alike.

An entry in the Auschwitz notebooks states that on October 23, 1943, a transport of seventeen hundred Jews from Bergen Belsen arrived in Auschwitz.[20] They were all gassed. What the German record omits is that among its seventeen hundred human beings were the aristocracy of Polish Orthodox Jews, including the daughter-in-law and the grandson of the world-famed rabbi of Gur.

It also does not state that they departed for Auschwitz dancing and singing, for it was the Jewish holiday of Simhat Torah. Also, among the seventeen hundred human beings on the transport was a Christian Pole. When the woman he loved, a beautiful Jewish girl named Estherke, was taken to the camp, he decided that freedom without her was meaningless. He joined her and was deported with her. All the passengers on that death train were holders of South American passports and classified as foreign nationals, who were supposed to be exchanged for Germans in Allied territories. Their train, instead of going to Switzerland, arrived in Auschwitz. When they realized that they were deceived, women from the transport attacked S.S. guards on the way to the gas chambers. This includes the famous episode of the killing of S.S. Oberscharführer Schildinger.[21]

If one is to be content with the German source alone, the train and its passengers remain anonymous, faceless ciphers: sealed cars with numbers chalked on their plank walls, entered in the *Auschwitz Notebook*, numbers chalked on again at the crematorium entrance, the number of victims inside the chamber and the time of gassing. Using this data alone is indeed a study of the extreme, of the absurd, but not of history.

The source and nature of Holocaust documents must be of primary concern, no matter what the particular interest is. Hannah Arendt's assessment of the Eichmann trial is, among others, an example of the use of one-sided historical data and the total absence of Jewish sources. Gershom Scholem was greatly disturbed by her conclusion of Jewish compliance in their own destruction. He wrote to her:

> In your treatment of the problem of how the Jew reacted to these extreme circumstances—to which neither of us was exposed—I detect often enough, in place of balanced judgment, a kind of demagogic will to overstatement.
> . . . with your earlier book in mind, I had expected something different.[22]

But even the historian eager to present a balanced historical account of the Jewish aspects of the Holocaust may find it a difficult task. It is not due to the overwhelming quantity of documents but rather to the scarce availability of primary source material. One needs first to locate the material, much of it still in private collections scattered in many countries, and, having once located it, to endow it with the respectability and creditability of an historical document. The process is a long one and an excruciating one. It is a deterrent for many. Yet it is the responsibility of the Jewish historian to follow through this painful process.

While history selects its own data, in its own process, as quoted earlier, it is up to the responsible historian to supply it with such data. This is the task of our generation, especially of the historian.

Bertold Brecht said that "imagination is the only truth." Perhaps he overlooked the fact that truth must also be based on accurate historical documentation.

Notes

1. For a survey of literature denying the Holocaust, see Joseph Elgazi in *Yalkut Moreshet* 28 (November 1979): 95–106.

2. Peter Gay, *Freud, Jews and Other Germans: Masters and Victims in Modernist Culture* (New York, 1979), p. 9.

3. *Choroba Glodowa: Badania Klinicze Nad Glodem Wykonane W Getcie Warszawskie. Z Roku 1942* (Warsaw, 1946).

4. Robert J. Lifton, "Medical Experiments in the Concentration Camps" (Paper delivered at the Fourth International Historical Conference: The Nazi Concentration Camps and the Condition of Jewish Prisoners, Yad Vashem, Jerusalem, 21 January 1980).

5. For a fine analysis of Styron's novel *Sophie's Choice*, see Alvin H. Rosenfeld, "The Holocaust According to William Styron," *Midstream* 25, no. 10 (December 1979): 43–49.

6. Yaffa Eliach, "The Hasidic Tale of the Holocaust," in *Proceedings of the Seventh World Congress of Jewish Studies* (Jerusalem, 1980), pp. 37–44.

7. Terrence Des Pres, *The Survivor* (New York, 1976).

8. Walter Kerr, *New York Times*, 13 November 1966, II:1:1.

9. Elie Wiesel, "Report to the President" (President's Commission on the Holocaust, 27 September 1979, p. iii).

10. It is of interest to note that among the few Jewish historians of the Holocaust period are historians of Eastern European origin: the late Philip Friedman, Jacob Robinson, Isaiah Trunk, Ber Mark, and Israel Guttman and Lucy Dawidowicz in Israel and the United States.

11. Zalman Gradovski, in *Megilat Auschwitz*, ed. Ber Mark (Tel Aviv, 1978), p. 188. The translation is my own.

12. Zalman Gradovski in *Aleph-Tav* 1, no. 3 (Spring 1975): 23.

13. Raul Hilberg, ed., *Documents of Destruction* (Chicago, 1971), pp. 47–55.

14. Shlome Farber, ed., *Olkeniki in Flames* (Tel-Aviv, 1962), p. 208.

15. Judg. 16:30.

16. See Shaul Barkli and Peretz Alufi, eds., *Eisyshok-Korotea Ve-Hurbana*, Hebrew-Yiddish (Jerusalem, 1950), pp. 57–66, 125–26.

17. Jews were first mentioned in Eisysky in the year 1145, and the tombstones in the old cemetery where the town's Jews were annihilated in September 1941 dated back to the thirteenth century! Eisysky was founded by the Lithuanian prince Eisys in 1070.

18. "My God, my God."

19. Yaffa Eliach, *Hasidic Tales of the Holocaust: Hovering Above the Pit* (New York, 1982).

20. *From the History of KL Auschwitz*, Panstwowe Muzeum w Oswiecimiu, 1967, 1:204.

21. Eliach, *Hovering Above the Pit*, tale no. 69.

22. Gershom Scholem, *On Jews and Judaism in Crisis* (New York, 1976), pp. 303, 306.

Christology and Jewish-Christian Relations

ROSEMARY RADFORD RUETHER

The anti-Semitic heritage of Christian civilization is neither an accidental nor a peripheral element. It cannot be dismissed as a legacy from "paganism," or as a product of purely sociological conflicts between the church and the synagogue. Anti-Semitism in Western civilization springs, at its root, from Christian theological anti-Judaism. It was Christian theology that developed the thesis of the reprobate status of the Jew in history and laid the foundations for the demonic view of the Jew that fanned the flames of popular hatred. This hatred was not only inculcated by Christian preaching and exegesis. It became incorporated into the structure of canon law and also the civil law formed under the Christian Roman emperors, such as the Codes of Theodosius (A.D. 428) and of Justinian (sixth century). These anti-Judaic laws of the church and the Christian empire laid the basis for the debasement of the civic and personal status of the Jew in Christian society that lasted until the emancipation in the nineteenth century. These laws were, in part, revived in the Nazi Nuremberg Laws of 1933.

The understanding of Christology is, I believe, at the heart of the problem. Theologically, anti-Judaism developed as the left hand of Christology. Anti-Judaism was the negative side of the Christian affirmation that Jesus was the Christ. Christianity claimed that the Jewish tradition of Messianic hope was fulfilled in Jesus. But since the Jewish religious teachers rejected this claim, the church developed a polemic against the Jews and Judaism to explain how the

25

church could claim to be the fulfillment of a Jewish religious tradition when the Jewish religious teachers themselves denied this.

At the root of this dispute lies a fundamentally different understanding of the Messianic idea that developed in Christianity, in contrast to the Hebrew Scriptures and the Jewish teaching tradition. Judaism looked to the Messianic coming as a public, world-historical event which unequivocally overthrew the forces of evil in the world and established the reign of God. Originally Christianity also understood Jesus' Messianic role in terms of an imminent occurrence of this coming reign of God. But when this event failed to materialize, Christianity pushed it off into an indefinite future, that is, the Second Coming, and reinterpreted Jesus' Messianic role in inward and personal ways that had little resemblance to what the Jewish tradition meant by the coming of the Messiah. An impasse developed between Christianity and Judaism, rooted in Christian claims to Messianic fulfillment and supersession of Judaism, that were not only unacceptable but incomprehensible in the Jewish tradition. The real difference between these two views has never actually been discussed between Christians and Jews in any genuine fashion because, at an early stage of development, these growing differences of understanding of the Messianic advent were covered over with communal alienation and mutual polemic.

Christian teachers sought to vindicate their belief in Jesus as the Christ by reinterpreting Hebrew prophecy to accord with the Christian view of Christ. This Christian exegesis also denied the ability of the Jewish teachers to interpret their own Scriptures. The Jews, Christians said, had always been apostate from God and their teachers spiritually blind and hard of heart. In effect, Christian theology set out to demonstrate the rejected status of the Jewish people and the spiritual blindness of its exegesis and piety in order to vindicate the correctness of its own exegesis and its claim to be the rightful heir of Israel's election.

According to Christian teaching, it is the church which is the true heir to the promises to Abraham. It is the spiritual and universal Israel, foretold by the prophets, while the Jews are the heirs of an evil history of perfidy, apostasy, and murder. As a result the Jewish people have been cut off from their divine election. Divine wrath has been poured down on them in the destruction of the temple and the national capital city of Jerusalem. They have been driven into exile and will be under a divine curse as wanderers and reprobates until the end of history, when Jesus returns as the Christ and the Jews finally have to acknowledge their error.

In effect, the church set up its polemic against the Jews as a historical task of Christians to maintain perpetually the despised status of the Jews as a proof of their divine reprobation. At the same time, the church taught that the Jews must be preserved to the end of history as "witness" to the ultimate triumph of the church. This theological stance was expressed in the official policy of the church toward the Jews through the centuries, combining social denigration with pressure for conversion. It also unleashed waves of hatred and violence that were seldom controllable within the official church policy of minimal protection of Jewish survival. In Nazism the Christian demonization of the Jew's spiritual condition was converted into a demonization of their biological condition. Hence the Nazi final solution to the Jewish question was not religious conversion but physical extermination, to make way for the millennium of the Third Reich.

For us, who live after the Holocaust, after the collapse of Christian eschatology into Nazi genocidal destruction, profound reassessment of this whole heritage becomes necessary. Although Nazis hated Christians as well as Jews, the church nevertheless must take responsibility for the perpetuation of the demonic myth of the Jew that allowed the Nazis to make them the scapegoat of their project of racial purity. This Christian tradition also promoted an antipathy in Christians, who too often felt little need to respond to the disappearance of their Jewish neighbors. We have to examine the roots of the theological patterns that fed this demonic myth of the Jew and its perpetuation, even in liberal theologies, today.

I propose to examine here three basic theological patterns that promote anti-Judaism. I will discuss how these dualistic patterns of Christian faith and negation of Judaism have operated historically. I will also present critical reconstructions of these theses, freed, it is hoped, from their anti-Jewish bias. Then I will focus on

Christology, as the center around which all these dualisms cluster, and ask how Christology itself has to be reconstructed in the light of these criticisms.

The Schism of Judgment and Promise

The Christian *Adversus Judaeos* tradition was built on a two-sided exegesis of the Hebrew Scriptures. On the one hand, Christian midrash of the Psalms and Prophets sought to show that the Scriptures predicted Jesus as the Christ, and also that they demonstrated the perfidy of the Jews and predicted their final apostasy. This exegesis was developed by Christian teachers before the written New Testament as a part of the oral tradition of Christian catechetics. It was incorporated into the exegesis and theology of the New Testament. The argument continued as a proof-texting tradition into the patristic period. Writings against the Jews in the corpus of the church fathers continued to be built on a tradition of christological and anti-Judaic proof texts. This exegetical tradition shows the close connection between Christology and anti-Judaism.

This type of exegesis fundamentally distorted the meaning of prophetic criticism. The dialectical structure of prophetic thought was split apart, so that its affirmative side, of forgiveness and promise, was assigned to the Christian church, while its negative side, of divine wrath and rejection, was read out against the Jews. This splitting of the left hand of prophetic criticism from the right hand of hope and promise creates an unrelieved caricature of evil projected upon another people with whom the Christian no longer identifies. The church, divorced thereby from the heritage of prophetic self-criticism, stands triumphant and perfect. The Hebrew Scriptures, which actually contain the tradition of Jewish religious self-criticism and repentance, are turned into a remorseless denunciation. All the evils condemned by the prophets are seen as characteristic of this perfidious people. Anti-Judaism and ecclesiastical triumphalism arise as two distortions of a false polarization of the prophetic dialectic.

This ancient Christian tradition of exegesis has practically disappeared among Old Testament scholars. Most Christian scholars of Hebrew Scripture interpret them historically, and not as predictions of Jesus as Christ. This also leaves largely unexplained the theological claim that the New Testament "fulfills" the Old (the term Old Testament itself, of course, reflects a christological and anti-Judaic interpretation of Hebrew Scripture).

A more difficult problem occurs in the New Testament. Here anti-Judaic exegesis has been woven into the very patterns of theological interpretation and put into the mouth of Jesus himself. I will confine my remarks to the denunciations of the scribes and Pharisees that occur in the synoptic Gospels. I suggest that we see here two different stages of development. In the first stage, in the ministry of Jesus, there is a denunciation of hypocritical religion that stands in the authentic line of Hebrew prophecy. As the prophet Amos cried out against externalized ritual:

> I hate, I despise your feasts,
> and I take no delight in your solemn assemblies.
> . . . .
> Take away from me the noise of your songs;
> to the melody of your harps I will not listen.
> But let justice roll down like waters,
> and righteousness like an ever-flowing stream,
> [Amos 5:21, 23–24]

so the Jesus of the synoptics cries out:

> Woe to you, scribes and Pharisees, hypocrites! for you tithe mint and dill and cummin, and have neglected the weightier matters of the law, justice and mercy and faith; these you ought to have done, without neglecting the others.
> [Matt. 23:23]

Such denunciations are not rejections of Judaism but are built upon Judaism itself. They presuppose Hebrew faith and existence within the covenant of Israel. The Matthew passage does not in any way reject the Torah. It stands within the debate of rabbinical schools of Jesus' time about the priorities for interpreting and following Torah.

A second stage occurs when the Christian church comes to perceive itself as a fundamentally new covenant founded on the new way of salvation, Christ, that supersedes the Torah and renders it obsolete and inferior. Then the prophetic critique of hypocritical ways of living the law come to be read as a denunciation of the law itself as *essentially* hypocritical. The criticism of bad scribes and Pharisees is taken to be a rejection of all Jewish scribes and Pharisees as essentially teachers of this bad religion rejected by Jesus.

The shift from one to the other may appear subtle, but in fact it is fundamental. In contemporary terms it would be the difference between a person who denounces a patriarchal reading of Christology and a person who denounces Christology as essentially patriarchal and calls for all people who desire justice to leave the Christian church and found a new religion based on a different soteriological principle. The first person remains within the Christian tradition, however many Christians may find what is said unacceptable. The second person has chosen to reject the Christian community as a context of identity.

The Jesus who announced a coming reign of God and preached to the poor in a manner critical of religious elites was undoubtedly a radical and controversial figure, but not one who stood in any way outside the Jewish tradition. Contemporary Jewish scholars have no difficulty affirming this Jesus as a part of the spectrum of Jewish controversy over the law and the kingdom in the first century. But the Christ of Christian faith, whose Messianic hope has been translated into a supersessionary principle over against the Torah, is a figure that departs fundamentally from the ground of peoplehood in Israel. He has become the basis of an anti-Judaic gospel.

There is no way to retrace this historical path and assume literally the stance of Jesus as prophetic critic and Messianic proclaimer in the Judaism of his day. If the 970 million Christians were suddenly to apply to reenter Judaism, the 14 million surviving Jews would certainly not know what to do with us. Rather we must reconstruct the stance of Jesus in a way appropriate to our own historical condition.

There are two elements in a correction of the anti-Jewish reading of Jesus' criticism of religion. On the one hand, we must recognize that prophetic criticism is always internal criticism, a criticism that springs from loyalty and commitment to the true foundations of the people whom you criticize. It is fundamentally distorted when it becomes simply the repudiation of another people who are no longer your own. Therefore whatever is valid in the denunciation of legalism and hypocrisy in the Gospels must be appropriated by Christians as self-criticism. We must translate words such as *scribes* and *Pharisees* into words such as *clerics* and *theologians*. Since most of us who have the chance to do that are ourselves clerics and/or theologians, it should be evident that what is being criticized is not Christianity or even Christian leadership but certain false ways of setting up leadership that crushes the message of the gospel. We might remember that Jesus himself was called rabbi by his apostles.

This kind of internalization of the gospel critique of religion is already quite common in Christian theology and preaching. Many liberal and liberation theologians, such as Hans Küng or Leonardo Boff, put particular emphasis on this denunciation of false religion precisely for the purpose of criticizing fossilized hierarchical religion within their own religious communities.

However, this internalization of the gospel criticism of religion will not overcome the anti-Judaic stereotype unless we are willing to concede to the Judaism of Jesus' day the same religious validity that we attribute to our own Christian faith. Surely we expect our own religion not only to survive but to be purified through such criticisms. If Hans Küng does not think that he becomes anti-Catholic because he denounces hypocritical hierarchicalism in the Catholic church, then he should not assume that Jesus fundamentally departs from the ground of Torah and Israel when he makes a similar denunciation of false teachers.

This second principle is seldom observed by Christian scholars. Again and again we find Christian theologians, not just conservatives but theologians on the Left, who are happy to use the gospel denunciations to critique legalistic tendencies in their own community. And yet they continue to write as though these bad traits, which are only *distortions* of their faith, are somehow *generic* to Judaism. Indeed such anti-Judaism becomes reasserted and defended by liberal and liberation thinkers as though the purging of the shadow side of their own faith still demanded the Jewish scapegoat as its point of reference.

This negative projection of Christian self-criticism onto Judaism cannot be corrected without a positive appreciation of Judaism, of the rabbinic tradition and Jesus' place in the Judaism of his time. Christians must discover that leaders of the Pharisaic schools, such as Hillel, were making some of the same interpretations of the law as did Jesus, that is, that love of the neighbor is the essence of the law. Christians must correct the stereotypic use of the word *Pharisee*. Only then will Christian exegetes and preachers be prepared to translate the New Testament language into the same kind of nuanced appreciation of Jesus' Judaism that they would expect to convey about their own Christianity; namely, a religion that contains the possibilities both of prophetic vision and of institutional deformation.

The Schism of Particularism and Universalism

Christians have seen their faith as the universal religion, superseding the particularism of Judaism. Paul's "neither Jew nor Greek" is seen as the great breakthrough from tribal religion to the religion of universal humanity. Christianity fulfills the Messianic promise of the ingathering of all nations, as opposed to the particularistic identification of Israel with one people and one land. It is true that particularism, even in the Hebrew Scriptures, sometimes becomes simply ingrown ethnocentricity and animosity to others. But what has been less apparent to Christians is the way that universalism can become imperialism toward all other peoples. Christianity has seen itself as the *only* valid, redemptive identity. All other religious identities are seen as spurious, demonic, and lacking true relationship to God. To be saved, all must incorporate themselves into the one true human identity, the Christian faith. Even modern liberal theologians, such as Bultmann, speak of Christianity as "authentic humanity" without asking whether this means that all other peoples have an inauthentic humanity. The missionary who viewed non-Christians as devil worshipers did not always avoid translating this theological judgment into a racial judgment on the inferior nature of non-Christian peoples. The mandate to conquer and subdue all nations often went hand in hand with the mandate to convert all nations.

Such imperialist universalism fails to be authentically universalist. It actually amounts to the absolutization of one particularism. In this respect Christianity can learn something from the very different way in which Judaism has understood universalism. Judaism has seen itself as having a universal mission to enlighten other nations about higher religion, expressed particularly in monotheism and the basic code of ethics, that is, the Noachian code, as distinct from the Torah. Although Judaism is open to the true proselyte, it has not seen its mission primarily as conversion of others to Judaism. This is both because Judaism sees its special characteristics as given to a particular people rather than to all people and also because it believed that the "righteous Gentile" could be saved in his or her own religion. Conversion to Judaism is not necessary for salvation. These views lay the basis for a self-limited particularism that, potentially, recognizes the rights of other peoples to define their own identity and relation to God in terms of their own religious culture.

True universalism must be able to embrace existing human pluralism, rather than trying to fit every people into the mold of religion and culture generated from one historical experience. Only God is one and universal. Humanity is finally one because the one God created us all. But the historical mediators of the experience of God remain plural. There is no final perspective on salvation available through the identity of only one people, although each people's revelatory point of reference expresses this universal in different contexts. Just as each human language points more or less adequately to universal truths, and yet is itself the product of very particular peoples and their histories, so religions are equally both bearers of universal truth and yet particular in form. To impose one religion on everyone flattens and impoverishes the wealth of human interaction with God, much as imposing one language on everyone steals other peoples' cultures and memories. If there is a Messianic "end point" of history that gathers up all these heritages into one, it can only happen through incorporating them all, not through suppressing them all in favor of the experience of one historical group. In order to be truly catholic, Christians must revise the imperialistic way they have defined their universality.

The Schisms of Law/Grace and
Letter/Spirit

Classical Christian theology brought together two kinds of dualisms, one inherited from apocalyptic Judaism and the other from Hellenistic philosophy. The apocalyptic dualism divided the Messianic people of the new age from a fallen and apostate history. The Qumran community, for example, saw themselves as the Messianic Israel of the age to come, over against the apostate temple and unconverted Jewish nation.

In the Hellenistic Jewish philosopher Philo we see an exegesis built on the dualisms of letter and spirit, outwardness and inwardness, body and soul. Philo himself did not translate this into a sectarian type of Judaism; rather he wished to give a sacramental understanding of Jewish laws and rites whereby the outward observances point to higher spiritual and universal truths. He did not negate the laws and rites themselves but enjoined fellow Jews to observe them with a new understanding.

The apocalyptic dualism of the Messianic community and the apostate Israel fostered polemic sectarianism. In the Dead Sea sect only the Qumran covenanters are regarded as the true Israel that will inherit the promises in the age to come. The apostate Israel will be cut off and thrown into the pit of fire. Yet the Qumran sect remained intra-Jewish. It sought to convert fellow Jews into its own community. Christianity originally probably shared this type of Jewish Messianic sectarian perspective. But as it became progressively gentile and alienated from fellow Jews, it translated this intra-Jewish sectarianism into an anti-Jewish sectarianism. Judaism became the alien religion and nation that had been superseded and negated by God.

The absorption of the Platonic dualism of letter and spirit into the sectarian apocalyptic dualism allowed Christianity to define itself over against the old law and covenant. The old covenant and law are seen as only the "fleshly foreshadowing" of a redemptive truth which is now fulfilled on a higher spiritual plane in Christianity. Christianity is seen as superseding Judaism, not only historically but morally and even metaphysically. Judaism becomes only letter, fleshliness, and carnality, over against Christianity as spirit and grace.

The fallacy here lies in confusing the break between two historical peoples with the theological line between history and eschatology. The distinction between ambiguous historical existence and perfected Messianic life is imported into history to define the line between two peoples and two historical eras. Israel as the harlot people (which, in the Old Testament, expressed critical historical realism) is used by Christianity to depict the Jews only in negative terms over against the perfectionist version of the church as the Messianic bride of Christ. This results in a mystification of Christian reality. Christians project the shadow side of human life onto the Jews as the symbol of the fallen and unfulfilled side of human existence. We find here a polarization of two sides of a dialectic, which makes sense when applied to one community but creates a completely distorted perspective, both for oneself and for the others, when split into two peoples and two "eras."

Judaism is not only "letter," any more than Christianity is only "spirit." All religions, indeed all human cultures, are a complex dialectic of letter and spirit, faith and law. Religious renewal always wishes to make the content, the inner experience, predominant. But this never takes place without mediating community structures, patterns of prayer, creed, liturgy, ethics, and community life. Christianity has certainly not been without all these embodiments. Indeed, ironically, its constant search for renewal of the inward experience means that it has proliferated far more "embodiments" of itself than any other historical religion. But it has also mystified the relationship between the spirit and the institutional embodiments, either trying to deny historical embodiments, as in charismatic movements, or else idolizing its historical, institutional form as perfect and divinely given. Christians have yet to develop a realistic account of the relativity, yet necessary relationship, between inward content and historical embodiment.

Christian churches have also tended to proliferate the supersessionist view of historical relationships. Not only is Christianity seen as superseding Judaism, but each renewed church sees itself as superseding its parent church. The new church is the true church of spirit and faith over against the old church of dead letter and rote ritual. This same supersessionist pattern has also been projected into the secular doctrine of progress. "Progressive" peoples see themselves as superseding and rendering obsolete "unprogressive" peoples. We must criticize this supersessionist view of historical relationships between groups.

We can indeed value and affirm those breakthrough experiences of human life that allow new groups to arise and to develop new historical identities that are authentic and fulfilling. But this does not mean that the religion or nation from which this group has departed becomes superseded in some absolute way. They may be discovering, at that very same time, a way of renewing themselves on the basis of their traditional symbols and forms that is equally authentic. Thus Christianity, at the very period when it was shaking the dust of Judaism off its sandals, failed to notice that Judaism was undergoing a creative renewal. Indeed it was the Pharisees who refounded Judaism after the demise of the temple and laid the basis of rabbinical Judaism.

Christianity, as much as Judaism, continues to live in a dialectic of fulfillment and unfulfillment. Christianity, in the resurrection, looks back to a foundational experience that expresses hope and conquest of defeat. Judaism, which did not participate in this particular experience, continues to renew itself out of the experience of the Exodus, which mediates much the same message. For each, the hope mediated by the breakthrough experiences of liberation is the basis for a continued struggle for the final resolution to the riddle of history that is as much ahead of us Christians as it is ahead of the Jews.

The supersessionary pattern of Christian faith distorts both Jewish and Christian reality. We should rather think of Judaism and Christianity as parallel paths, flowing from common memories in Hebrew Scripture which are then reformulated into separate ways that lead two peoples to formulate the dialectic of past and future through different historical experiences. But the dilemma of foretaste and hope remains the same for both. For both live in the same reality of incompleted human existence itself.

The Key Issue: Christology

The anti-Judaic patterns of Christian theology were and are still today tied to a dogma of fulfilled Messianism. So it is not possible to rethink these anti-Judaic patterns without questioning its christological basis. There are two necessary steps in this critique of Christology.

First, Christians must formulate the faith in Jesus as the Christ in terms which are proleptic and anticipatory, rather than final and fulfilled. Jesus should not be said to fulfill all the Jewish hopes for the coming Messiah, which indeed he did not. Rather he must be seen as one who announced this Messianic hope and who gave signs of its presence, but who also died in that hope, crucified on the cross of unredeemed human history.

In his name we continue to proclaim that hope, and also to begin to experience its presence. But, like Jesus, we also do that under the cross of unresolved human contradictions. The final point of reference for the Messianic advent remains in the future. Its unambiguous arrival still eludes us. Here and now we, as much as the Jews, struggle with unresolved history, holding on to the memory of Jesus' resurrection from the cross as the basis for *our* refusal to take evil as the last word and *our* hope that God will win in the end.

This proleptic understanding of Jesus' Messianic identity is familiar to Christian exegetes. It has been particularly renewed in liberation theologies. It is the exegesis that best translates the New Testament experience. Jesus' message is falsified when it is translated into a final fulfillment that is spiritualized and institutionally lodged in the past.

Second, we must see Christology not only as proleptic but also as paradigmatic. We must accept its relativity to a particular people. This will be a more difficult principle for many Christians to accept, but it is equally inescapable. The cross and the resurrection are contextual to a particular historical community. These are breakthrough experiences which found *our* people, that mediate hope in the midst of adversity *for us*. But this does not mean that these are the only ways that this may happen, or that other people may not continue parallel struggles on different grounds, for example, the Jews, for whom the events in Jesus did not become paradigmatic events, and who continue to found themselves on the Exodus and the Torah as the memory and the way.

Some Christians will see such contextualizing of the Christian symbols as totally unacceptable. For them, Jesus as the only name that may be named on earth and in heaven is absolute. I can only say that our two thousand years of human experience do not allow that assertion to be taken literally. He may indeed be the only name *for us*. But other names continue to be named and do not fail to bear fruit. Nor does it seem to me that the power of Jesus' name will become less if we cease to use that name to deny the validity of other people's experience of God through other means. Indeed, only when we cease to use Jesus' name to negate other people's experiences of the victory of life over death can the name of Jesus cease to be a name that creates alienation of Jew from Christian, Christian from non-Christian. Instead we can begin to find in our differing ways of mediating hope in the midst of defeat new possibilities of human solidarity.

The German Church Struggle and Its Aftermath

JOHN S. CONWAY

A few months after the end of the Second World War, in October 1945, in the bombed and devastated city of Stuttgart, a meeting was held of the surviving leaders of the German Evangelical churches, including Pastor Martin Niemöller, recently released from seven years imprisonment in the Sachsenhausen and Dachau concentration camps. They issued a now-famous declaration addressed to "The Christians in Other Lands" which stated:

> With our people we know ourselves to be not only in a community of suffering, but also in a solidarity of guilt. With great anguish we state: through us inestimable suffering was inflicted on many peoples and lands. What we have often witnessed before our congregations we now declare in the name of the whole church. Indeed we have fought for long years in the name of Jesus Christ against the spirit that found horrible expression in the National Socialist regime of force, but we charge ourselves for not having borne testimony with greater courage, prayed more consciously, believed more joyously, and loved more ardently.[1]

This declaration, the first legacy of the German Church Struggle to be mentioned here, caused and still causes great controversy. To some it did not go far enough. It lacked concreteness. It said, for example, not a word about the terrible fate of the Jews at the hands of the Nazis, or about the failure of the churches to oppose the Nazi racial doctrines. It gave no specific indication for the future or suggestions as to how the lessons of the German Church Struggle were to be incorporated into the postwar world. Apprehension was expressed by a critical minority of church leaders lest this Stuttgart "Declaration of Guilt" be regarded as a kind of alibi and the task of real repentance and reformation avoided. These fears have been largely confirmed in subsequent years.

To the vast majority, however, the Stuttgart declaration went far too far. Germany lay defeated and divided, physically ruined and morally humiliated. What right had these church leaders to pronounce the guilt of Germans without mentioning the responsibility of other nations? In the grim circumstances of postwar survival, the general mood was to seek to lay the blame on others, in particular of course the Russian Communists and their ill-fated Western allies. The call for national repentance and a new start fell on deaf ears. Instead German church leaders, both Catholic and Protestant, adopted the widespread phenomenon of collective amnesia about their part in the Nazi era. Refuge was taken in the exculpatory explanation that the German people as a whole had not known of the Nazi excesses, or that they had been silenced by the all-powerful might of the police state. It quickly became convenient to claim that the blame should be laid on Hitler and his satraps, whose "demonic" force had captured the state apparatus and crushed all potential source of resistance.

In these circumstances, the conservative majority wished to regard the Nazi era as an unfortunate episode in German history. This was reflected in the constitutional arrangements for the postwar church, which restored the 1932 church polity almost intact. The restoration mood also applied to the power of the individual congregations and to the relationship between the church and the state. The Catholic church, for example, maintained its privileges as gained by the Reich Concordat of 1933, and the tradition of a hierarchically organized and heavily bureaucratic church government was only enhanced by the refusal to abandon the highly advantageous system of church financing. Doubtless these moves reflected the similar tendencies in the secular political field when, under Adenauer's leadership, the West German Federal Republic was established along conservative restoration lines. The churches attempted to portray themselves as the inheritors of Germany's better traditions and as such were supported by the Western allied military governments. But such moves doomed the efforts of those who believed that the impulse of the Church Struggle was to establish a new church, free of the state ties, whose vitality and independence would be guaranteed solely by the vision of its professed adherents. The attempt to carry forward the Confessing Church as a prophetic minority, dedicated to being a "church for others," along the lines indicated by Dietrich Bonhoeffer before his tragic execution, petered out in face of the general desire to return to the comfortable security of a national and all-inclusive *Volkskirche*.

It must be admitted that the task of coming to terms with the impact of the Church Struggle was not much helped by the historiography of the early postwar years. During this period, the majority of books about the Church Struggle were written by members of the Confessing Church, whose principal object was to justify their own policies in defense of their vision of the gospel and to denounce the heretical attitudes of those who had governed the churches during the Nazi era. But they were at pains to show that their opposition had been theological rather than political, and revealed that they were otherwise both nationalist and conservative in their attitudes. Hence the ambivalent policies of even the Confessing Church toward the Nazis in such matters as the restoration of Germany's national power, the invasion of Eastern Europe, and most significantly the persecution of the Jews. Furthermore these authors blurred over the record of their own former sympathies and their own participation in the political processes which had not only brought the Nazis to power but also sustained them after 1933. Instead, the attempt was made to depict the Confessing Church as resolutely opposed to Nazism, by men who now appeared as members of the "resistance" without defining clearly what kind of resistance was meant. The result was that a thoroughgoing examination of the deeper issues, both theological and political, was omitted. The impact of the Church Struggle was instead distorted to support the reestablishment and reintegration of the churches into a basically conservative society. In 1963, the eminent Swiss theologian Karl Barth could pertinently point to the "spiritual paralysis in the Evangelical church in Germany that began such a short time after the brief awakening during the time of the Church Struggle."

It was thus left up to a critical minority and some foreigners to ask more far-reaching questions and to suggest that the experiences of the German Church Struggle had significance not merely for Germany but for the whole church.[2] As Franklin Littell remarked,

> The heroic image of a tiny minority, valiantly and clear-heartedly resisting the Nazis, is like a well cultivated tropical plant of brilliant colour. There remain, however, a number of unsettled questions to which the vivid contrasts rather blind the eye. It may be that a certain amount of "demythologising" of the Church Struggle will be necessary before the true view begins to emerge.[3]

At the same time, we have also seen a useful "demythologizing" of the secular history of Nazi Germany over the past two decades. The simplified view that Hitler alone was responsible for the fatal course of developments or that he was solely interested in grasping power for its own sake has given way to a more sophisticated examination of the totalitarian experience. Today we are more fully aware of two significant phenomena of the Nazi state: First, the polycratism, or plurality of power structures, within the Nazi hierarchy, which was not such a monolithic police state that the individual was helplessly trapped and unable to oppose all Nazi policies or practices. Instead, we are now more aware of the rivalries and feuds within the Nazi party, which allowed scope for alternative strategies of resistance.

Second, historians have given the ideological factor much more prominence in recent years. Not only do we now realize the centrality of Hitler's anti-Semitism in his political career, but we can trace the importance of the ideological conditioning and manipulation of the population as a significant factor in the acceptance of Nazi totalitarianism.[4]

These developments have provided scope for more searching analysis of the German Church Struggle, particularly with regard to the questions of religiously motivated opposition to the state, of the structures required for an adequate defense of human rights, and of the role of the church in providing ideological underpinning for the society's cultural values.

We are now adequately informed, I believe, about the reasons for the German churches' enthusiastic endorsement of Nazi rule in 1933. I have myself suggested elsewhere four principal factors, namely, the ingrained tradition of pietism, the readiness to exact obedience to established authority, the influence of pseudo-Christian doctrines, and a doctrinaire anti-Communism.[5] To this may be added a fifth, the latent anti-Semitism of many church people, both Catholic and Protestant. More recently, Klaus Scholder in his splendid account of the early stages of the Church Struggle has drawn renewed attention to the baneful influence of the "political theology" propagated by such leading German theologians as Emanuel Hirsch, Paul Althaus, and Werner Elert. Their support of a nationalistic pattern of revelation, their opposition to any ecumenical or foreign contacts, and their explicit anti-Semitism certainly had a wide following. But it may well be argued that these characteristics were not merely descriptive of the German churches of the 1930s but present a real and continuing temptation to churches elsewhere, especially those which uncritically accept the kind of *Kulturprotestantismus* which identifies church and nation as equally valid bonds of loyalty.

Against these views the minority of the Confessing Church protested. They sought to restore the centrality of the lordship of Christ, not Hitler, and to recover the Word of God as normative for the church. As Eberhard Bethge has pointed out, their courageous stance in the totalitarian surroundings became not only a witness for, but even an organized stronghold of, freedom. It was in fact an island of nonconformism. But the German churches had no adequate tradition or theological preparation for nonconformity. Basically the Confessing Church never wanted to adopt this position and quickly abandoned it in the freer circumstances of the postwar world.

On the other hand, some theologians saw the legacy of the Confessing Church as lying in its protest against all forms of political engagement. In recent years a new movement has started up in Germany which seeks to oppose the present-day developments in the churches, and especially in the World Council of Churches.[6] For these persons, the "purity" of the gospel has to be maintained against any radical tendencies or theologies of adaptation. Here too, as any observer of the American Christian scene can see, the attractions of a creed supposedly free of politics or above parties, relying solely on "born-again" Christians, are by no means extinct. The antihumanistic, antipluralist, and even authoritarian overtones of this tendency should not be overlooked.

There have certainly been those who see the principal lesson of the Church Struggle as consisting in the need for the churches to strengthen their defenses. When assaulted by a hostile world, or totalitarian political forces, the church should retreat within the walls of the sacristy and raise the drawbridge against the infidels outside. This was particularly noticeable in East Germany in the immediate postwar years, when the shock of finding themselves under the unwanted rule of a Russian-dominated Communist government led many church people to see their church institutions as fortresses, or as outposts of a previous civilization, from which they hoped to be rescued by their Western brothers and sisters. It has taken many years for some of the more courageous leaders of the East German churches to overcome this negative, backward-looking stance. Instead they have sought to draw other lessons from the Church Struggle, and to learn that reliance on the church's traditional privileges was by no means the only way for it to live. Particularly in East Germany, Bonhoeffer's prophetic words were especially applicable. Writing from his cell in Tegel prison in the dark days of 1944, he looked forward to a time ahead:

> We may have to face events and changes that take no account of our rights. It will not be difficult for us to renounce our privileges, recognising the justice of history. But if so, we shall not give way to embittered and barren pride, but consciously submit to divine judgment, and so prove ourselves worthy to survive by identifying ourselves generously and unselfishly with the life of the community and the sufferings of our fellowmen.[7]

It has been the difficult task of the East German churches to incorporate these teachings into their daily life. The legacy here has been on the one hand to seek to claim the church's freedom to pronounce the word of reconciliation and redemption, and on the other to liberate the church from its past inheritance of domination and authoritarianism. It is perhaps noteworthy that the senior Evangelical bishop in East Berlin in recent years has been Albert Schönherr, one of Bonhoeffer's early pupils during the Church Struggle.

Mention of Dietrich Bonhoeffer brings us to one of the most controversial figures of the *Kirchenkampf*. His legacy has of course been preserved for us by the selfless and dedicated work of his friend Eberhard Bethge, the editor of the *Letters and Papers from Prison*, of Bonhoeffer's other theological works, and also the author of the outstanding biography, published in 1966. Throughout the last thirty-five years, Bonhoeffer has remained a challenging but much debated personality. To begin with, he was revered especially by foreigners, as a martyr for the cause. He seemed to symbolize the heroic resistance of the Confessing Church against Nazism, and his teachings undoubtedly gained much from his faithfulness even unto death.[8] In Germany, however, and even among the members of his own Confessing Church, his position was more equivocal. Bonhoeffer's participation in the conspiracy against Hitler could be regarded as high treason, and even to this day the German Evangelical church has refused to give its approval to such action. Bonhoeffer's martyrdom was for many too obvious a reminder of their own failure to resist the Nazi oppression or to seek to overthrow the tyrant whom they had so long praised as Germany's savior.

Bonhoeffer's example and his wrestling with the problem of justified resistance by the church to totalitarian oppression has however been widely noted in ecumenical church circles. For example, a recent document published by the World Council of Churches on the situation in South Africa recalled that "there have throughout history always been Christians who have for moral reasons deeply recoiled from the use of force, but who nevertheless have used force in order to bring an even greater evil to an end. One of the best-known examples in recent history is Dietrich Bonhoeffer's participation in the conspiracy to kill Hitler."[9] Others have gone further and sought to use Bonhoeffer as a paradigm for all church policy in the struggle for liberation, especially in Latin America, and have tried thereby to enlist him as a hero of guerrilla terrorism against the exploitative forces of capitalist imperialism.

Over the past thirty years, the debate in both the Catholic and the Protestant churches of West Germany over the questions of war, peace, rearmament, conscientious objection, and nuclear weapons has been both continuous and vigorous. Numerous, if highly divergent, overtones from the Church Struggle can be heard. Space will not allow me here to enter into the theological arguments advanced on all sides, though, as we could expect, these have been argued with typically laudable German thoroughness.

In the early 1950s, the majority of conservative Christians, both Catholic and Protestant, accepted Chancellor Adenauer's policies for Germany's rearmament and inclusion in NATO, justifying their position by reference to traditional doctrines of obedience to the state, or by arguments in favor of the need for defense against atheistic Communism. A vocal minority, however, led by Pastor Niemöller, sought to use the legacy of the Church Struggle as a means of arousing support against such policies, and instead campaigned for German neutralism or even pacifism. The church should not once again fall into the error of blindly supporting the political authorities but should actively "work for compromise rather than confrontation, for East-West contact rather than ideological isolation and for reconciliation rather than deepening division."[10] Niemöller was supported by one of Germany's leading Protestant politicians, Gustav Heinemann, who had himself played an honorable role in the Church Struggle, and who later went on to become President of the Republic. But this program, based on Christian pacifism and pro-reunification nationalism, proved to be an unconvincing combination. Neither of the major political parties was eager to enlist the Niemöller-Heinemann group to its side, and attempts to found a third party, the all-German People's Party, around Niemöller's Emergency League for the Peace of Europe failed to attract enough support to become a viable alternative. Niemöller and his friends courageously, though perhaps somewhat dogmatically, continued to campaign against compulsory military service, the adoption of nuclear weapons, and the hardening of attitudes toward the Soviet bloc. Their witness was undoubtedly motivated by a sense of repentance for the past and a longing for reconciliation with the East. Even though, in the main, they were unsuccessful in preventing the alignment of western Germany into the NATO alliance, their protest did lead to a significant and totally new accommodation for the rights of conscientious objectors. Perhaps even more significantly, the Evangelical church's 1965 memorandum on policies toward the East paved the way for the acceptance of the loss of the Oder-Neisse territories to Poland, and for a more open attitude toward both the Soviet Union and East Germany. This undoubtedly helped to prepare the ground for Willy Brandt's Eastern policies during his later chancellorship, by stressing the need for Germans to seek forgiveness for their crimes during the war and to regard the territorial changes as not only final but morally just.

The continuing influence of Karl Barth is still evident, not merely in his theological interpretations of the Church Struggle, but equally in his political attitudes, for example his sympathy for the political left wing, his suspicion of the Catholic church, and his antipathy toward America. As recently as the election of October 1980, certain circles in the Evangelical church, drawing on this legacy, raised questions about the moral and ethical policies of the present participation in the European Community, which is seen to be too closely aligned with the Catholic church, with multinational capitalist organizations, and with the continuing reluctance to support the cause of the underprivileged and the underdeveloped in both Europe and the wider world.[11] Not surprisingly, one of Niemöller's latest utterances, of May 1977, is entitled "Against the Europe of the Rich" and warns against the insidious idolatry of current West German materialism.

Further influences of the Church Struggle can be seen in four other developments: first, the erection of the Evangelical Academies, a series of conference centers with the deliberate aim of fostering in the church a more active political and social consciousness of contemporary problems; second, the establishment of the biennial series of church rallies, or *Kirchentage*, which bring together thousands of lay persons, especially young people, for a week-long meeting, out of which numerous new initiatives have been started;[12] third, the *Aktion Sühnezeichen*, a form of Peace Corps activity, deliberately designed to enlist young Germans to undertake practical works of reparation, especially in Israel and Eastern Europe; fourth, the Sisterhood of Mary, Darmstadt, the only Protestant order of nuns, founded by Mother Basilea Schlink in 1947, with an explicit mission of repentance for the omissions of the past.

Finally let me turn to one of the most significant areas impacted by the Church Struggle, namely the delicate and controversial attitude of the church toward the Jewish people. Although this issue has clearly been recognized as concerning the worldwide Christian churches, my emphasis will be on the German experience in the period since 1945. Five aspects or phases may be distinguished, which overlap chronologically according to the attitudes of the various church groups.

First, there was a slow acknowledgment of the burden of guilt. As mentioned, the Stuttgart "Declaration of Guilt" of October 1945 made no direct reference to the church's failure to espouse the cause of the Jews. In 1946 the Nuremberg trials first drew attention to the centrality of the Jewish persecutions in Nazi planning, but even there the full enormity of these crimes was not spelled out. We should remember that at that time Auschwitz was barely mentioned, and it was to be several years before the realization sunk in as to the full extent of the Holocaust. Some German church leaders, such as Bishop Marahrens of Hanover in 1946, could acknowledge that the ill-treatment of the Jews was morally wrong, but he saw this purely as a human failure, as a faulty means for dealing with a legitimate problem.[13] And a statement of the Council of Brethren of the Evangelical church in Germany issued in April 1948, while calling for repentance for the past, could still adopt a triumphalist view of the relationship of the church to Judaism. In April 1950 the synod of the whole Evangelical church at last recognized that a much clearer call for the acknowledgment of guilt was needed. As one of the members, Pastor Kreyssig, declared, "In every train which carried Jews to their death-camp in the East, at least one Christian should have been a voluntary passenger."[14]

This acceptance of personal guilt was matched by full support for the policy of *Wiedergutmachung*, reparation as far as possible to the survivors and their relatives or to the newly created state of Israel. But there was still only a minority who recognized that this first aspect had to be complemented by a far more thorough rethinking of Christian theological attitudes, beginning with an examination of Christian complicity in anti-Semitism.

This second phase began to be widespread only in 1961, when

the revelations of the Eichmann trial were followed by the creation of a new commission for the relations between Christians and Jews which was set up by the Evangelical church and attracted a large following at the 1961 *Kirchentag.* This commission was quickly apprised of the need to see the relations of the church and Judaism as a central issue. The Christian complicity in prewar anti-Semitism demanded not only the abandonment of previous prejudices but a searching revision of Christian theology. Slowly the realization grew that the Holocaust was not merely something which happened to the Jews. It was, as Franklin Littell has called it, a Christian event and raised excruciating questions about the credibility of Christianity.

The continuing work of this commission has helped to bring about a clearer sense of the fateful impact of Christian anti-Semitism before 1945. It is no longer possible to believe that the Holocaust was organized by Germans *despite* the Christian churches, or solely by Nazis besotted with racist ideologies drawn from anti-Christian sources. German Christians have been helped to realize their complicity through the contributions of foreigners, such as Rosemary Ruether,[15] Uriel Tal,[16] Franklin Littell,[17] and Richard Gutteridge,[18] but this phase is still far from complete.[19] German Catholics have also been slow to take up this theme or to realize its dimensions, though the pioneering studies of Gertrud Luckner, who initiated the valuable annual *Freiburger Rundbriefe* and was herself a hero of the Church Struggle, deserve mention.

The third aspect has been the search for new forms of Christian-Jewish dialogue. A post-Auschwitz theology which will rethink such fundamental issues in theology as the nature of God's calling and election of his people, the role of the Messiah, the legacy of St. Paul, and the controversial question of mission is now under way. Despite some efforts made to show that Bonhoeffer was implicitly already grappling with these theological issues during his last years,[20] it would be too much to claim that the Church Struggle as such prompted these significant reevaluations.

The fourth aspect was introduced by the establishment of the state of Israel. As mentioned, German church leaders welcomed this development and supported it politically. Only slowly however was its theological significance accepted.[21] Here again the new insights are too recent to be ascribed to the influence of the Church Struggle. But certainly the enormous wave of sympathy for Israel at the time of the 1967 war, as evidenced in many German churches, was a positive witness to the fact that German church people had learned the lesson that they could not once more be silent when the very lifeblood of Jews was threatened.

The fifth phase, in which we now stand, is more ambivalent. Since 1967 there can be no doubt that the political complexity of Middle East developments has produced many crosscurrents. The position of the Palestinian refugees and minorities in Israel has raised difficult questions. Bonhoeffer's legacy of seeing the church as serving the oppressed has led some church people to regard these people as sharing the same fate as other victims of political repression. The church is called to raise its voice of protest against the inhumanity of established powers, to support the cause of freedom and liberation, just as it sought to do, if weakly, forty years ago. Such a witness must therefore also be proclaimed, perhaps even more necessarily, in the holy land of Israel. I think we can expect considerable controversy over this particular aftermath of the Church Struggle.

Let me conclude by suggesting two salient points. First, the German Church Struggle should not be seen as merely a historical event which can be safely relegated to the history textbooks. The issues then raised, especially with regard to Christian anti-Semitism, have relevance today. Nothing in the subsequent generation can lead us to believe that the abuse or misuse of state power against which the Confessing Church protested has grown less dangerous or threatening to the values for which Christians and Jews alike stand.

Second, the German Church Struggle was not just a German event. Had it been solely concerned for the defense of the German churches' position and privileges, the overthrow of Nazism in Germany and the restoration of the pre-1933 situation might have sufficed. But at the time, alert church leaders, especially in the ecumenical movement, were aware of its wider significance. Since 1945, the realization has grown that the ongoing collapse of every credible religious and moral restraint on the state, the extraordinarily powerful force of propaganda, the growth of dehumanizing ideologies of various kinds, and the erosion of religious traditions which were so evident during the Nazi era, and against which a part at least of the Christian church protested, were and are sinister and fateful developments which are by no means confined to Germany. Perhaps the principal impact of the German Church Struggle is to force us all to face these facts with more courage and with more faith.

Notes

1. *Kirchliches Jahrbuch 1945–48*, ed. J. Beckmann (Gütersloh, West Germany, 1948), pp. 26–27.

2. See, for example, for the Catholics, Guenther Lewy, *The Catholic Church and Nazi Germany* (New York, 1964); Carl Amery, *Die Kapitulation* (Hamburg, 1963); Hans Müller, *Katholische Kirche und Nationalsozialismus* (Munich, 1963); Gordon Zahn, *German Catholics and Hitler's Wars* (New York, 1962); for Protestants, Klaus Scholder, *Die Kirchen und das Dritte Reich*, vol. 1 (Berlin, 1977); J. R. C. Wright, 'Above Parties', *The Political Attitudes of the German Protestant Church Leadership 1918–1933* (Oxford, 1974); Franklin H. Littell, *The German Phoenix* (New York, 1960); Eberhard Bethge, *Dietrich Bonhoeffer* (Munich, 1966); and my own *The Nazi Persecution of the Churches 1933–1945* (London, 1968).

3. Franklin H. Littell, "Current Study of the Church Struggle with Nazism and Its Significance for Church History" (Paper delivered at the spring meeting of the American Society of Church History, Southern Methodist University, April 1960).

4. For a more extended treatment, see John S. Conway, "The Historians and the Holocaust," *The Annals of the American Academy of Political and Social Science* 450 (July 1980): 153–64.

5. See John S. Conway, *The Nazi Persecution of the Churches 1933–1945* (London, 1968), pp. 334–37.

6. See particularly W. Künneth, *Der Grosse Abfall* (Hamburg, 1947), and *Das Neue Rotbuch Kirche* (Stuttgart, 1978).

7. Dietrich Bonhoeffer, *Letters and Papers from Prison*, ed. Eberhard Bethge, enl. ed. (New York, 1972), p. 299.

8. For example, George Bell, bishop of Chichester, in a memorial address in July 1945: "Bonhoeffer's death like his life, marks a fact of the deepest value in the witness of the Confessional Church. . . . He and his fellows are indeed built upon the foundations of the Apostles and Prophets. . . . For him . . . there is the resurrection from the dead . . . for the Church, not only in that Germany which he loved, but the Church Universal which was greater to him than Nations, the hope of

a new life," as quoted in Eberhard Bethge, *Am gegebenen Ort: Aufsätze und Reden* (Munich, 1979), p. 162.

8. World Council of Churches, *South Africa Today: What Price Hope?* (Geneva, 1978).

10. For a full discussion of this debate, see Frederic Spotts, *The Churches and Politics in Germany* (Middletown, Conn., 1973), pp. 241ff.

11. For example, see G. Casalis, "Nicht religiösen Glaube heute," in *Konsequenzen*, ed. E. Feil (Munich, 1980).

12. For a full account, see Littell, *The German Phoenix*.

13. Richard Gutteridge, *Open Thy Mouth for the Dumb: The German Evangelical Church and the Jews 1879–1950* (New York, 1976), p. 300.

14. Kreyssig, as quoted in Gutteridge, *Open Thy Mouth*, p. 303.

15. Rosemary Radford Ruether, *Faith and Fratricide: The Theological Roots of Anti-Semitism* (New York, 1974); Ger. trans. *Nächstenliebe und Brudermord: Die theologischen Wurzeln des Antisemitismus* (Munich, 1978).

16. Uriel Tal, *Christians and Jews in Germany: Religion, Politics and Ideology in the Second Reich 1870–1914* (Ithaca, N.Y., 1975).

17. Franklin H. Littell, *The Crucifixion of the Jews* (New York, 1973).

18. Gutteridge, *Open Thy Mouth*.

19. For German works, see references in G. B. Ginzel, ed., *Auschwitz als Herausforderung für Juden und Christen* (Heidelberg, 1980), especially the article by Rolf Rendtorff, "Judenmission nach Auschwitz," pp. 539ff.

20. See Eberhard Bethge, "Dietrich Bonhoeffer und die Juden," in Feil, *Konsequenzen*, pp. 171ff.

21. See Clemens Thoma, ed., *Auf dem Trümmern des Tempels: Land und Bund Israels in Dialog zwischen Christen und Juden* (Vienna, 1968); W. P. Eckert, N. P. Levinson, and Martin Stöhr, eds., *Jüdisches Volk-Gelobtes Land* (Munich, 1970).

Religious Values After the Holocaust: A Protestant View

ALLAN R. BROCKWAY

In addressing the topic at hand I should like to begin with two autobiographical recollections.

I am a Depression baby. That is to say that I was born in 1932, the year that Franklin Roosevelt was first elected to the presidency of the United States. When President Roosevelt died, just before the end of the Second World War, I was almost twelve years old.

The significance of this otherwise irrelevant fact is that I am a member of a generation that is neither fish nor fowl, that remembers the war but knew nothing of it. I remember asking my father what the radio newscasters talked about when there wasn't a war. He replied, "They read recipes." In particular, I knew nothing of the Holocaust at the time it was going on; if any mention of the mass murder in Europe was made on those newscasts, I don't remember it.

I do remember collecting tinfoil for the war effort and saving my nickels to buy stamps at school to go in the book that would, when filled, become a war bond. I do remember ration stamps (my mother could never get enough sugar for canning) and the scarcity of other items, such as rubber for automobile tires. But the war did not consciously touch me in my childhood; I knew it was going on, I had no doubt about the Allies' ultimate victory, but it caused me no anxiety and certainly no hardship.

The values I incorporated during those years were the standard so-called Protestant values of frugality, diligence, church attendance, personal piety, and patriotism. I knew nothing of what I came later to call racism, though the "values" of racism were ingrained in me with the air I breathed. The question of anti-Semitism was never raised; to my knowledge no Jews lived in the small town where I was growing up during the war. But, of course, I knew quite well what "the Jews" had done to Jesus and absolutely nothing of what "the Christians" had done to "the Jews."

No one thought much about the events of the Second World War in the high school I attended, and I learned nothing of the Holocaust there, or in college, in any intentional way. Indeed, it was not until 1953 when, for a contemporary literature course, I read John Hersey's powerful novel *The Wall*, about the Warsaw Ghetto, that I was introduced to any knowledge, much less feeling, about the Holocaust. I shall always be grateful to Hersey for the awakening, all unbeknown to him, of a young man about to enter the ministry of what was then the Methodist church.

Now again, the only relevancy of this recollection lies in the fact that it took me so long, and then by accident, to begin to comprehend what had happened only a few years before. As I look back on it now, Hersey's novel did for me what some young people now testify the television series "Holocaust" did for them: it told me that the values I had taken for granted, the values of respect and honor for human life and for the dignity of the individual, were not historically absolute values: they could be—they had been!—flouted, denied, and indeed totally rejected.

The second of my autobiographical recollections comes from about fifteen years later, when I was editor of a social action magazine of the Methodist church. At the time of the 1967 Arab-Israeli War I wrote and published a short editorial in which I suggested that Jews need never worry—in the future the United States and the world would not allow Israel to be pushed into the sea. Along with other Protestant editors, I was immediately called to task by my Jewish colleagues for those too little, too late, and unconsciously insensitive words. And I began to realize, in a way I had never before, that still I had been taking for granted that the values I had learned as a child were inviolate, at least in the United States and the Western world. And that I had not even begun to learn the lessons of the Holocaust.

The horror facing us today is that the Holocaust actually happened, that it happened in *our* world, the world of all those values I was taught as a child. But the additional horror is what I began to learn—and am still painfully learning—after the 1967 war. That is that some of those values, if made paramount, endanger other vital values. In brief, religious and religiously motivated patriotic values have the power to override humanistic and humanitarian values. Let me explain.

The distinction that Karl Barth made between religion and faith, which I learned most explicitly through Dietrich Bonhoeffer, who wrote about "religionless Christianity," has yet to make its way fully into our thinking about values. But the Holocaust says nothing to us if it does not insert that distinction indelibly into our collective consciousness. For it was the preeminence of religious values that produced the Holocaust, religious values that forced humanistic and humanitarian values into a secondary and finally nonexistent role. These latter, the humanitarian values, I wish to argue, are at the heart of the Christian value system based on faith, but they are foreign to religion, Christian religion in particular. The former, the religious values, were at the heart of Hitler's final solution.

It is true, of course, that Hitler's religion was not Christianity, despite his formal allegiance to Catholicism. Instead, his was a religion founded on race and blood, that fed upon the historic pragmatic religion of Christianity. But it was religion, nevertheless, because it placed idealistic, event transcendent, values above those of human beings and of peoples. Hitler demonstrated in the most horrible fashion imaginable that religious values made absolute are demonic.

Christianity has been prone, more than most religions, to just such demonism. Torquemada's Inquisition is a beautiful example, during which Jews and others were made to "confess" Jesus Christ or suffer painful deaths. The people, the individuals, were unimportant; what happened to them as persons made no difference. The only things that mattered were the transcendent values of the religion. But Hitler took the religious value system one crucial step further. For him, religion was not a matter of belief, it was a matter of being. "Being precedes essence," the existentialists have told us, but for Hitler being and essence were identical. If a man or woman was "Aryan," this was sufficient for salvation (literally). Otherwise, particularly if one were a Jew, one's essence denied existence—and it was the Nazi religious duty to actualize that denial of existence, which is, of course, just what the death camps did.

It has often been noted that, had the "final solution of the Jewish question" been totally successful, and had the war not been lost, Hitler would have set about the systematic extermination of Christians as well. There is nothing inconsistent about that. For though Christians' "essence" was not so readily identifiable as that of Jews (which wasn't all that easy to identify either, as the Nuremberg Laws testify), if someone was defined as essentially a Christian, then that someone had no business being in existence. It is not hard to imagine some system comparable to Torquemada's being utilized by the Nazis to effect "conversion" of otherwise "Aryan" people to Hitler's religion. And through it all, the fundamental values of Christian *faith*, though not necessarily Christian religion, were in the process of being obliterated.

What I am pointing toward is the critical difference between values integral to faith as opposed to values integral to religion. The values of religion, are, first and foremost, those that promote the religion. In other words, the religion itself is the primary value and all other values are subsidiary. Thus, if the religion requires that human beings be sacrificed or otherwise slaughtered, then that must be done. Any insistence that human beings have intrinsic value is brushed aside, not only as a nuisance but as idolatry.

The history of the Christian religion is replete with illustrations of the deleterious effect of its sometimes more and sometimes less complete institutionalization within society. But institutionalized Christianity has always been tempered by the faith it bears. It took the absolutism of the Nazis to demonstrate the genuine implications of consistently applied religious values. And what the Nazis demonstrated was that when religious values are carried to their logical conclusion, they deny the values inherent in both Christian faith and humanistic reason.

It is instructive to note that Hitler did not generally imprison, murder, or otherwise persecute those who were merely adherents of the Christian religion (*Deutsche Christen*). But he fully recognized the danger from those of Christian faith. These latter refused not only to participate in the expression of the Nazi folk religion but, more importantly, actively held to the values of their own faith, values that could never be harmonized with those of the Nazi regime and religion.

What were, and are, those values? They are what might be called horizontal values, those that make real, live people more important than abstractions, more important than religious belief. The value system of Christian faith does not differ from that of any enlightened humanist, it should be observed, save in one important particular: Christian faith is grounded in the conviction that active dedication to the infinite worth of the created universe in general and specific human individuals in particular is the first, last, and only test of one's faith in God. No one loves God who does not love those loved by God—which includes every single human being, of whatever color, belief, nationality, sex, or age. Nothing could have been farther from the Nazi creed. And nothing could be farther from the Christian religion when religion takes precedence over faith.

I need not chronicle again the dismal record of the Christian churches and the majority of individual Christians when confronted with the fact of Hitler's mass murder of their friends and neighbors—the Jewish business people, secretaries, accountants, homemakers, factory workers, schoolteachers, laborers, and children of Europe. What is important for us to note today is that there was little in the history of the Christian religion to prompt a response other than that of the *Deutsche Christen*. For centuries the church had taught that the Jewish people had been written out of God's plan of salvation. It was not merely a peripheral religious tenet; it was central to the Christian religion itself, for from the earliest days of the church religion had displaced faith.

We can see, for instance, that in Luke-Acts the church came to view itself as a kind of new people, a third racial grouping between Gentiles and Jews. This meant that the Jewish people and the pagan world had no future. Only the church had some kind of destiny. This is an interpretation voiced especially by Professor Gregory Baum. It requires no stretch of the imagination to make that read: The Nazis saw themselves as the third race beyond Jews and Christendom. By implication this position negated the future of the Jewish people and the Christian church. Only the Aryans had a destiny. And the Aryans possessed the political and military power, like the church beginning with Constantine, to develop the social implications of their religious doctrine. Because theirs was an unrelenting religious belief, they became one of the few unambiguously religious societies in all of history. Hitler and his minions were nothing if not consistent.

The Christian religion, bereft of faith, fell easy victim to the Nazi religion, for especially when it came to the Jewish people, there was little difference between them at the level of belief. The principal difference was that whereas the church remained the bearer of Christian faith despite itself, there was no vestige of such affirmation of the human individual within Nazism.

But we might say, what if the theology, the religion, of Christianity had put priority on the intrinsic worth of individual human beings? That question and its answer are of greatest concern for us today, for the fact is that seldom, if ever, has the hypothetical coincidence of religion and faith existed. Throughout history, religion has tended to emerge supreme in the lives of peoples and nations.

Lest I be accused of suggesting that there are no differences among religious values, that they are uniformly demonic, let me issue a denial in advance. Many, if not most, religious values do not conflict in the least with the fundamental divine affirmation of the temporal and ultimate intrinsic worth of individuals, as both persons and peoples.

Indeed the values of community, which support mutual aid among community members and even for the "stranger within the gates"; of allegiance to and worship of the transcendent Creator, Sustainer, and Redeemer of humanity and the entire created universe; of personal and corporate prayer and adherence to life styles that correspond to it—all these values of religion are also the values of faith.

Where religion begins to separate itself from faith is when

particular understandings of the transcendent Creator, of prayer, of community, and so forth, become absolute in opposition to differing understandings and it becomes necessary (or so it is thought) to defend the religion against those others. Moreover, when religion believes—and acts on the belief—that it must convert others to its own system in order to be true to itself, then it has separated itself from faith. This latter, of course, has been a failure, one might even say sin, of Christian religion. In sum, the values *of* a religion are not necessarily what I am calling religious values. There is a great difference between practicing a religion and adhering to a religious value system.

Once that has been said, however, the question remains as to whether it is possible for the values of faith, the values centered on the infinite, indeed cosmic, worth of each human individual, to become normative for societies in this post-Holocaust age. Are the values of faith up to the task of guiding the actions of peoples and societies?

Ours is a world in which it is not possible for any of us to live in isolation from others within our own society or from others in societies on the other side of the globe. It is a world that forces decisions upon us that we would much prefer not to make. And it is a world that is placing almost unbearable pressure upon the value of the human individual.

There are, for instance, too many people in the world, and the number continues to grow. Most of this population growth is taking place among people who are Hindus, Buddhists, Muslims, various kinds of "primal" religionists, and of no readily identifiable religious identity at all. In addition, the resources available to the enlarging world population are not growing at anywhere near the pace of the population itself. Technology, once thought to be the guarantor of a new age of plenty, has fallen before the scarcity and cost of natural resources to fuel its computers, airplanes, and machines of war, not to mention its air conditioning, petroleum-based fertilizers, and automobiles.

The question persons of faith face today is a new one in human history; at least it is new in terms of the greatness of its dimensions. That question is, which human beings are to be affirmed when not all human beings can possibly be preserved?

59

Who is to say who shall live and who shall die? What criteria shall be used for such "awe-full" decisions? The faith statement that *all* people are, by definition, of infinite value turns out to be a criterion by which everyone is damned if you do and damned if you don't. But the alternative is infinitely worse.

In face of this kind of radical pressure upon a world society that emerged scarcely yesterday in historical times, we are witnessing the reemergence of religious solutions, solutions which, from the perspective of faith, deny the validity of human beings as individual people. Today the most obvious of these reemergences is seen in the Islamic "fundamentalism" in Iran, Afghanistan, Pakistan, and other nations of the Near and Middle East. But it is also present in the religiously based policies of Israel and the equally religiously based attitudes and actions of the United States and the nations of Western Europe. With the exception of those in places such as Iran, these religious solutions are not usually framed in explicitly religious categories, but they are religious nevertheless, for they repair to supposedly transcendent values for their justification of a refusal to place determining value on individual people—real, live, individual human beings. Instead, what we see referred to are Islamic law, biblical tradition, and human rights, the last of which has become an extremely flexible category for support of those who will conform to United States policy. People are killed for the "holy" cause of religion; religion becomes a mockery of faith.

What the Holocaust should have taught us is that religion, no matter what its form, leads to hatred, destruction of people (who are individuals with their own hopes and dreams and daily lives), and governmental forms that institutionalize that hatred and destruction.

The Jewish people has much to teach the rest of us in this turbulent world about the danger of religion, despite the present religious determinism that characterizes the Israeli government. The Talmudic insistence upon the primacy of not doing to others what one would not want done to oneself is, of course, central to Christian faith (though certainly not to Christian religion, as the history of the church gives ample evidence). Judaism has not been principally a religion. It has been and is a people, a people that understands itself to have been chosen by the Founder of the world to be a "light to the nations." The world has, of course, not accepted that people as such. Instead, it has seen that people as a threat, as an anachronism that inexplicably preserved itself into the modern world, that should not have survived—but nevertheless did survive—not only the destruction of the second temple but also the onslaught of Nazism. The guilt of the Western world and the guilt of Christendom have not been able to overcome the fundamental threat that the mere existence of the Jewish people represents for Christian religion and for the secularism that has overcome the Western Christian world.

Secularism, properly understood, is synonymous with Christian faith when it comes to the affirmation of the intrinsic worth of human individuals. But the secular world and its system of values fails, in the last analysis, because it is unable to root its value system in anything that transcends itself. After all is said and done, it simply will not do to assert that human beings are valuable because they think they are. A value-laden *cogito ergo sum* is nothing more than a nihilist cry.

So I am back to my initial autobiographical observations. I was a child during the war and thus during the Holocaust. Clearly I have no responsibility for what went on then. I didn't kill any Jews. I didn't acquiesce in the death of a single Jew. By the time I became aware of the death camps, they were long gone. No one can blame me for either positively killing Jews or not taking action to prevent their death. I'm innocent, am I not?

I wish it were so. I am an adherent of the Christian religion. I'd like to say that I live in Christian faith and nothing else, but the truth of the matter is that Christian faith cannot exist without Christian religion. I want, desperately, to deny Christian religion and affirm Christian faith apart from the religious value system that Christianity enforces. But I cannot. The best I can do is live and act for Christian faith within the Christian religious system. So I, like most other sensitive Christians, fight against the religion and try to affirm the faith, for the most part without success.

The Holocaust stands over against our religious systems. It stands as a mute testimony against all our protests that we are not responsible. When all the evidence is in, and the evidence now available is almost more than one can stand, the demand for *metanoia*, for repentance, for going in a new direction away from religion toward faith, on the part of Christians—whether they live in the so-called Western world or whether they live in the so-called Third World—remains. The values of the Christian faith focus on human beings, no matter their religious identity, nationality, or race. Every one is infinitely valuable.

So we reject the Nazi values. So we reject the values of religion, which, when pursued to their logical extreme, end up in Nazi values. We still are left with a world in which too many people live, in which nationalist, economic, and ideological values prevail.

The Holocaust tells us that faith in human and biblical values is extremely fragile. But it is a faith worth pursuing, a faith worth reinforcing, a faith worth our trust. For without it the future of the human species is less than dim and individual hope is hopeless.

Religious Values After the Holocaust: A Jewish View

IRVING GREENBERG

Orienting Events as Revelation

Revelatory events are central to Judaism and Christianity. Revelation means more than commandments or that the Word of God has been given to people. Revelation means more than that the events tell us something normative. The ultimate revelation model in Judaism and Christianity is that certain events are *orienting*. They bring humans into contact with a reality beyond themselves; that is, they reveal that behind the mundane, everyday reality (which appears to be so factitious and self-contained) is a ground that nurtures its life and value and gives it direction. When this ground is in itself unknowable—or at least cannot be exhaustively known—the orienting event reveals its presence. The event sets the goals and directions of the religion, that is, the way which is compatible with the hidden and (now revealed) ultimate nature of the universe. The event gives the fundamental guiding parameters for the believing community as it walks the way to the final goal—hence it is orienting.

Retelling or reenacting the orienting event is the central liturgical act of the religion. Reenactment accomplishes three things. It recalls the event, thus giving the faithful a renewal of strength to persist, to go on living by its insights. They are inspired not to yield to those recalcitrant, unredeemed everyday realities which resist the ultimate direction and obscure the underlying divine reality with their external facticity. The re-presented event gives the guidelines to the faith people to correct and cross-check their paths and actions along the historical way. The event is like a screen through which one checks and filters out the significance and appropriateness—that is, the ultimate compatibility with final value—of the behavior and methods developed along the way. Most daring of all, Judaism and Christianity suggest that reenactment makes the original event actually present again, overcoming the barriers of time, making it available to everyone who chooses to enter into it. Thus each generation is given access to the radiant energy and revelatory forces of the original moment.

Judaism's core is based on a central revelatory event—the Exodus. Out of this experience of liberation of the Hebrew slaves, by word of God and by hermeneutic, both initially and over time, came the fundamental directions of Jewish religion. Underlying the world is a God who cares; the ultimate fate of humanity will be redemption. One day all will live in a world where the dignity of humans in the image of God and the divine presence will be actualized. The contradiction between, on the one hand, evil and death in the reality and, on the other, the infinite life and value behind this reality will be overcome. The final revelation will shed retrospective light on the original one. The final revelation will come in the moment when the underlying reality of redemption will be manifest in, and at one with, the visible, daily world. Thus revelation will no longer be needed to uncover and reveal the hidden: all will be clear and known—all shall be prophets (Joel 2:28 [3:1 in MT]).

Christianity develops out of another central orienting event— the life, death, and resurrection of Jesus Christ. Out of this experience, and under the impact of further events, the Christian faith came into being. The revelation—Jesus' life—was understood as a further illumination of the levels of meaning in the initial orienting event of Exodus. In the eyes of the church which emerged, Jesus' life and history pointed to the same goal as the original covenant, that is, to redemption, but the parameters and way to the goal were drastically changed.

The sociopolitical Kingdom of God was not achieved by the end of Jesus' life. By the light of the new event, the understanding of the kingdom was transformed. The Kingdom of God was drastically internalized; the way to it was an inward journey. Indeed, the persistence of evil after Resurrection almost broke Christianity loose from history. It led to a discounting of the sociopolitical realm and a focus on the spiritual. In the final analysis, however, Christianity affirmed that in a Second Coming the world would be perfected, politically, economically, and socially, even as the spiritual perfection which was unfolding through the church's work would be completed.

The implications of the death and resurrection of Christ were understood to open up the covenant to the Gentiles. This turned the faithful into missionaries who traveled over land and sea to bring the good news to the entire world. The logic of the new orientation also suggested dropping many rituals and specific commandments in Judaism. In time, the cognitive dissonance between the ongoing people of the original covenant who did not accept the new event as orienting and the conclusions drawn by Christians led to the Christian conception of a New Covenant. The new event so overshadowed and displaced the old that despite a sense of continuity, those continuing to orient themselves by the old understanding were deemed to be following a false path, a misunderstood revelation.

The concept of later events orienting the way of redemption is intrinsic to Judaism. The Jewish quarrel with Christianity was not over the denial of possible successive revelatory events. The quarrel was over which was the further event. The birth and death of Jesus were not accepted as orienting for Jews. In that very same first century, however, the destruction of the temple was experienced as further revelation, that is, as an orienting event that changed the fundamental understanding of the covenantal way and gave guidance along the road still to be traversed (see below). The Exodus event, being the heritage of Jews and Christians, deeply affected Christianity and, through it, the world. The Destruction had a fundamental effect on Judaism, but not being assimilated in Christianity (except insofar as it was deemed confirmation that God had renounced the covenant with the original Israel), it had considerably less effect on the church.

Orienting events are religious models and find particular resonance in the sacred history (*Heilsgeschichte*) of Judaism and Christianity. However, in the course of the emergence of secular history—particularly in the past three centuries—other historical events have attained orienting stature in general culture. Although the culture denies universal claims of divine authority, it has been shaped and reshaped in its values by certain events. These events have been recognized as normative, and their internalized implications have reshaped religion, including Judaism and Christianity, as well as general cultural values. The Industrial Revolution, the democratic revolutions (English, French, American), the Russian Revolution, among others, have had normative effects far beyond their own borders and among people who would not use the language of divine revelation.

In this century, two events have occurred which because of magnitude and aftereffects bid fair to be orienting events in Judaism and Christianity and in modern culture itself. They are the Holocaust and the rebirth of the state of Israel. By guiding and redirecting people and culture, orienting events lead to reshaping of values. In this paper, I will focus on the Holocaust as orienting event and some of its implications.

The Holocaust as Orienting Event

Unfortunately, genocide is not new to human history. However, never before did a state decide to wipe out every last person of another people wherever they might be found—for the "crime" of being—even if they had no contact with that state. To this extent, the Nazi decision to kill all the Jews, which led to the Holocaust, may be differentiated from the model of the first twentieth-century genocide—the Turkish massacre of the Armenians. The Turks sought to kill or banish all Armenians in Turkey. Those who left were not hounded to their new lands, nor were any plans made to kill all Armenians, if and when they fell into Turkish hands, in the lands of their dispersion. To the Nazis, it made no difference what were the activities or behavior patterns of the victims or if they—or even their parents—had left membership in the Jewish people. Despite a history of persecution, Jews had never before been condemned to death universally with no possible remission or exculpation. The total nature of the Nazi decision suggests that a new cultural factor is operating, that is, a tendency unique to modern culture of functioning by universal and comprehensive categories. (Heinrich Himmler scornfully pointed to the party members who endorsed the annihilation program, but "then they all come trudging . . . each one has his one decent Jew [to exempt].")

Once the decision to kill Jews was taken, it was carried out with almost complete success in a manner designed to degrade and dehumanize the victims first and to devalue them even in death. Of course, the decision to kill was in itself an assault on values. Still, while killing went on all the time, the pattern of actions planned for Sabbath and Jewish holy days is so repetitive that it cannot be ignored. The Babi Yar shootings occurred on Rosh Hashana, the closing of the Warsaw Ghetto on Yom Kippur, the beginning of mass deportations on Tishah b'Ab, the final liquidation of the Warsaw Ghetto on Passover, and so on, and so on. The schedule of the destruction, roundups, and killings goes beyond murder and makes clear that a conscious assault on the sanctums of Judaism was intended as well. As the work of Uriel Tal and others demonstrates, there were strong religious/theological overtones, however perverted, in the Nazi ideology and in the attitude toward Jews. The "final solution" was the expression of the search for a final perfection through destroying the "anti-Christ," that is, the anti-perfection force incarnated in the Jewish people. Theological, directional ideology demands trampling or disproving the sanctums of the other, not just elimination of the victim.

All this was carried out by a highly civilized, cultured people with a high educational level and was made possible by the apathy or bystanding indifference of the democracies and of other religious groups and religions. As such, the event is a shock to the understandings and assumptions of the leading value systems of the West, that is, both modernity and the religions of Christianity and Judaism.

The Challenge to Modern Culture

Among the fundamental assumptions of modern culture was the idea of progress, in particular the move toward moral perfection.

Increased human power was the key to that progress. Scientists and industrialists stressed that productivity and technology would free humanity and increase the general welfare. Many scientists taught that science, untrammeled by religious authoritarianism, would produce a better world and free the human mind at the same time. Medicine promised that human control would end the scourge of disease. Psychology and psychoanalysis offered the hope that human power to take full responsibility would end the psychological crippling of humankind. Thus Freud argued that freedom from God would make possible human maturation and some perfecting of society even as Marx taught that ending belief in God and religion would cut off the supply of opium for the masses and make possible economic and social liberation. Social scientists argued that as rationality and science dissolved the web of custom and hierarchy that enclosed people, this would both liberate the individual and improve the human condition. All agreed that the growing individuation made possible by these developments was part of a general increase in human welfare and betterment of humankind's state.

All these assumptions are radically challenged in the Holocaust. Would that the Holocaust were an atavism, a throwback to the old German paganism, or a deviation from contemporary culture. While the Holocaust is a pathological outburst which flouts many of the basic values of modernity in crucial ways, it was made possible by this culture. Past persecutions of Jews were much more limited by technical difficulties. It took a massive technology of transportation and production to make possible the continuing mass murder that added up to six million Jewish dead. As Henry L. Feingold put it, "The 'Final Solution' utilized the industrial processes and the managerial techniques which enabled European civilization to dominate the world."[1] Raul Hilberg, Uwe Adam, and other scholars have shown the centrality of bureaucracy and impersonal bureaucratic procedures to the process of carrying out the Holocaust successfully. In past persecution such as the Crusades, the explosion of religious hatred which led to killings soon burned itself out once it was blooded. Eichmann and the other administrators of the final solution prided themselves on not hating Jews. The S.S. even set up courts officially for the purpose of punishing corruption or excessive abuse on the part of the S.S. camps administrators. While in fact an enormous amount of abuse went unpunished, the underlying idea was that this was an idealistic process, administered with integrity, and not an outburst of hate. The sense that this was a job enabled the bureaucrats to do their work with zeal and efficiency and with self-image intact. "To have stuck this out and . . . to have kept our integrity," said Himmler, is a "page of glory" in S.S. annals. In the mass killings carried out in hate, exceptions were granted personally. In the Holocaust, bureaucratically defined universal categories swept all Jews into the net of death. Thus the universalist orientation of modern culture—its mind-set to operate by rationalized, universal categories rather than by personalized and particularist relational categories—yielded a racist murder philosophy which would make no exceptions.

We now understand that the very processes which made possible the extraordinary achievements of industry, technology, and mass society also make possible unlimited death dealing. The side effects are far more deadly than anticipated.

Like a massive weight thrown onto supporting beams, which suddenly stresses and brings out flaws hidden beneath the surface, so the Holocaust also brings out challenges to two other key modernist assumptions. Certain universalist norms (respect for law, the common weal of society, universal legal responsibility for all, respect for individual life) failed to operate to check the killing of the Jews. Yet these same norms operated to disarm or expose the victims. The denial of group interest led to the creation of Jewish groups lacking prepared leadership and defense structures. The universalist ideology blocked recognition of the distinctiveness of Jewish fate and interest. In the early days of mass deportations in Warsaw, the socialist Left resisted any move to immediate armed revolt because it wanted to act primarily in concert with the Polish working class (that is, the general body of humanity as defined by Marxist ideology). So powerful was modernist ideology that the victims could not believe that this was being done in the twentieth century—and could not take appropriate evasive action.[2] The claim of the overall good (that is, prosecuting the war effort to its maximum) was used as the excuse not to bomb the death camps or to make special efforts to save the Jews. Thus we see that the universalist claims of modern culture—unless checked or limited by the insights gleaned from particularist outside cultures and their own interest—endanger the survival of minority or powerless groups. Yet the power of the universalist norms is their overriding particularist claims for exception. Again, modern culture's best values evoke their own moral nemesis.

The same must be said about the individualism which is so powerfully unleashed in this culture. The assault on the organic society, the dissolution of ethnic and communal bonds by the rationalism and self-interested individualism of modern culture, and the consequent freeing of the individual from fixed social and economic positions have generated great achievement and mobility. Therefore, these forces have been perceived as liberating, life enhancing, and individuating. The powerful sweep of Nazism, the appeal of totalitarianism, the search for "salvational" wholeness through the *Führer,* the total nature of the S.S. group, and the ideology of totalitarianism (including willingness to do everything commanded —to wipe out the "foreign bodies" to achieve the new "wholeness") suggest that the dissolving and individualizing tendencies of modern culture turn pathological when they reach a certain intensity or spread. Individualizing forces invoke their own nemesis, a reaction toward totalitarianism, surrender of self, a search for wholeness that is willing to totally destroy all that is perceived as standing in its way.

This does not mean that modernity must be written off or that it is the only cause of the Holocaust. Rather it implies that the working principles and values of modernity must be challenged, revised, and purged of their extreme tendencies so that they will stop nurturing elements that make for a Holocaust. Similarly, the testimony that modernity qua culture offers to the greatness and goodness of the human, progress, and so forth, will not be credible unless the statements take into account the offsetting testimony of the Holocaust event. Insofar as Judaism and Christianity have themselves undergone modernization processes due to the impact of modern culture, these modifications must be challenged and reviewed, along with modernity itself. Stanley Hauerwas has already argued that the universalizing tendencies internalized from modern culture led Christianity to become a *Kultur* religion, a camp follower of modernity, unable to make its believers see the direct conflict of values going on and the need to dissent totally from the destruction process being unleashed. The new balance of particularism and universalism which Hauerwas is urging is precisely the kind of reconsideration—rather than simple rejection—which is needed.

The Challenge to Tradition

The same challenge is faced by Judaism and Christianity. Both are religions of redemption; both proclaim a God who cares and the preciousness of the human in the image of God. Both are covenanted religions, predicated on the concepts of divine initiatives and redemptive acts and human committed responses and ways of living in order to advance and participate in that salvation. The Holocaust is a total assault on all these statements. It is countertestimony which undercuts the persuasiveness of both religions and contradicts the hope which they offer. Thus the absolute worthlessness of Jewish life in 1944 (children were burned alive to save one-half of a cent's worth of gas) is the devil's testimony to the lack of value in the human. Similarly, the degradation of the humans in the camps testifies that the human is a thing to be used up. In the words of Primo Levi, the mussulmen (prisoners in final state of disintegration) form "an anonymous mass . . . of non-men who march and labor in silence, the divine spark dead within them . . . one hesitates to call them living; one hesitates to call their death, death."[3] God's nonintervention during the Holocaust suggests the absence of a covenantal partner or a breakdown of covenantal responsibility. The fact that Christian anti-Semitism is implicated in furnishing ground for the hatred which was exploited to set up the Jews for victimization; the apathy or hostility of Christians during the Holocaust; the participation by people who considered themselves Christians or, at least, God-believers, in the mass murder process all strike further at religion's claims. In short, Judaism and Christianity can go on (and many in both faiths have gone on) testifying as if nothing had happened, but this erodes their credibility. It risks turning both religions into empty Pollyanna assertions, credible only because believers ignore the realities of history.

Furthermore, fundamentalist Christianity is correlated with nonkilling of (or nonresistance to killing) Jews on the part of local populations.[4] Particularist religious values discouraged taking ethical responsibility to stop ongoing destruction. (Cf. the response of the Catholic church and of Evangelical Protestants in Germany.) In light of this, the failure of certain wings of Judaism and Christianity to undergo modernization must be challenged and reviewed.[5]

This is not to suggest that the Holocaust supplies a new set of values or answers or that it simply wipes out the existing traditions. One must beware of using the Holocaust in univocal fashion, thus turning it into propaganda. By and large, its impact is dialectical: it is paradoxical and contradictory in its implications, tormenting in the irresolvable tensions it generates. This suggests that our task is to reshape values, passing them through the crucible of the flames of Auschwitz so they emerge shattered and re-fused. The test of authenticity is the increase in the capacity to resist a repetition and the ability to testify in a way that takes into account the implications of the Holocaust. The force of the Holocaust's impact shatters the certainty which undergirds all sets of values. At the same time, it forces a reconsideration of the direction in which people have been going, both in the faith communities and in the general culture. By revealing unanticipated side effects of modernity's own strengths, by highlighting the limitations and weaknesses of traditional religions, the Holocaust evokes a search for a new pattern. As I hope to show in the sections that follow, the impact of the Holocaust leads not so much to a change of ultimate direction as to a change in the manner and approaches to getting to the final ends. The Holocaust sheds light on the earlier pattern of the religions and the general culture even as it leads to some redirection of tactics and of paths. The reshaping of values constitutes the recognition of the Holocaust as orienting event.

Reshaping Values After the Holocaust

Modernity

Given the incredible destructiveness of the gigantic forces unleashed by modern culture which are exhibited in the Holocaust, religion, ethics, and philosophy must respond by a new thrust toward setting limits on human power. Component elements would include a critique of science and technology, a challenge to excessive individualism, and reaffirmation of communal and group roots as well as restoration of access to the transcendent.

In the course of unfolding modern culture, the transcendent has steadily been reduced or "domesticated." In many areas of social science, religion and God were treated as pure projections of the human condition. The thrust of historical studies also was reductionist or tending to insist that only encounters with the divine fitting the norms of philosophy and science could be credible. The net result was that sanctums and values all too often became human defined, finite, and temporizing in their demands. The transcendent capacity to challenge the given or make a dissonant demand was whittled away. In the light of the Holocaust, it can be recognized that this was setting the stage for the absolutization of anthropocentric values and norms. This process weakened a major source of alternative values and of judgment of human acts and authority. Access or channels must be opened for the incursion of the divine from the outside, beyond human-domesticated sanctums. We need to reconnect to a transcendent that is not simply manipulable by human culture, indeed one that demands resistance to the absolute claims of humans.

Of course, there are those who would claim that such a transcendent does not exist. The task of philosophy and thought is to remove the obstacles to such incursion; to release the stranglehold that checks those options of the spirit so that even if such contact occurs, it is explained away or denied. When the denying categories lose their absolute character, then the possibilities of the transcendent open up again.

The cultural change needed is a complex, sophisticated process. Its components would range from social movements for the conservation of earth's ecology that challenge the old societal blank check for technology all the way to Wittgensteinian and language philosophies that cut scientific truth claims down to relative rather than absolute dimensions. The limits of reason—as established by everything from psychoanalysis to sociology of knowledge—must be delineated. This process can break the tyranny of modern categories and allow a new dialectical relationship to the claims of reason and science. This is not a matter of simply going back to tradition. It is more like a movement toward postmodernity. An example: a postmodern biblical scholarship would move beyond historicist reductionism of the authority claims of Scripture and beyond an apologetic affirmation of the Divine "unsullied" by human history to the recognition of the profoundly historical nature of the divine metaphor, language, and presence in history. Religion cannot be unaffected by history (this is implicit in the influence of the Holocaust on theology), but it dare not be totally absorbed into cultural categories and relativized, lest it lose the power to oppose the extraordinary and total powers assumed by modern political and moral philosophies. Part of Christians' failure to resist the Holocaust was due to the conversion of Christianity to a *Kultur* religion whose practitioners were superloyal to the state and government.

Power

The extraordinary concentrations of power made possible in modern culture have shifted the balance of power enormously toward the oppressors. In many cases, they now have the power to break the will of their victims collectively and individually, to break their capacity for martyrdom or resistance, or to rob their death of significance even as martyrdom. In the crunch, the good will even of good people (for example, Franklin D. Roosevelt, Stephen Wise, Pope Pius XII) proved inadequate to the task of stopping the destruction, or unwilling to try. Therefore, a fundamental of ethical/political culture must be the reversal of the moral devaluation of power both in the secular modern tradition and in Judaism and Christianity. Absolute powerlessness corrupts even more than absolute power. Dislike of power must be shifted to an affirmation of (and active involvement in) the transferring of power to potential victims. This implies an affirmation of the legitimacy of group interests within a context of a universal society and the need to preserve strong ethnic and group loyalties and structures.

This is the rationale behind the Third World revolts and women's liberation. Oppressed groups came to see that the availability of extraordinary power concentrations in the modern world leaves them exposed to total annihilation and that they cannot depend on the good will of others for their basic dignity and right to exist.

This is why the Jewish people became overwhelmingly Zionist and fiercely committed to the state of Israel after the Holocaust.

To enter into a world of power ethics is to waive prophetic expectations of purity and ideal standards and to engage in guilty, partial accommodation, to link absolute ends and proximate means. Those who judge power on an absolute standard are guilty of unreal thinking; those who hold Israel to such a standard, ignoring or slighting the security risks and hostile environment it faces, are guilty of anti-Semitism as well.

Nor is this meant to be a blank check for power—or for Israel. Power is corrupting. Power exercised by erstwhile victims may be just as oppressive as that exercised by their old masters. Often nonoppressor status is a function of lack of power, not of lack of will to persecute. Therefore, those who support a shift in power will want to resist giving any moral blank check to former victims, including Jews. They also will want to support the widest distribution of power so that the balance will operate to check excess and encourage moral behavior in the rulers. Prophetic stances and demands for absolute morality are legitimate—but as commentaries or checks rather than as guides to basic political behavior. Thus again the reshaped principles are dialectical rather than a simple substitution of a new set of values for old. The recognition of the legitimacy of group interests must be offset by a strengthening of the overall universal norms to prevent degeneration into pure selfishness or the law of the jungle. On the other hand, the old idealist universalist ideology must not be allowed to choke off the individual group's self-assertion. This interest will become the basic module of political behavior which through a process of negotiation, shifting alliances, and controlled conflict will create an overall synthesis of meeting needs and sharing life.

Given the enormous force of ideology backed by power, and the unlimited evil it can do once in power, the "messy" way of compromise, pluralism, middle of the road must attain a new level of respect—as a check to potential Holocaust. Purity is a dangerous drug—to be used with great caution in political settings. Hitler had enormous appeal on university campuses in the early thirties as a relief from the bourgeois, compromised (admittedly, not too effective) politicians of the other parties. Similarly, perfectionist paradigms must yield to partial and process models as the mainstream of religious as well as political activity. In a way, the record of the Holocaust suggests that the central paradigms of perfection are "cracked" or shattered by this event. This accounts for the negative or destructive effects of purity—including pure perfectionist drives. Compromise and pluralism are more than tactics—they are more congruent with the revelation of a flawed core of history and life which the Holocaust as orienting event demonstrates.

Religious Testimony

In a world where children are burned alive to save gas, any speaking about God and divine concern should be done with great restraint. The fact that Heinrich Himmler insisted that all S.S. men believe in God ("otherwise they would be no different from the [atheistic] Marxists") only sharpens this point. The reorientation of religion in light of the Holocaust suggests that we are entering a time of theological silence. The best testimony that religionists can give (be they Jewish or Christian) is to restore the image of God to the world—by increasing life and/or by making it more precious and unique in accordance with its status as image of God. The presence of the image itself is the most credible testimony. It silently points to the unspoken presence of the Lord who is its model. Having a child is an extraordinary act of faith. The strength to create life wells up out of a Messianic love that overcomes destruction and defies death in the conviction that redemption can be created and achieved.

Since the scene of creation or enhancement of the human is primarily in the secular realm, religious groups must seek to participate in and redeem the secular. Similarly, past deviations in any of the traditions from the recognition of the full dignity of others (be they women, non-Jews, non-Christians) are much less supportable. As it were, the countervailing testimony of the Holocaust is so threatening to religious claims that any vitiation or weakening of the religious testimony threatens to totally tilt the balance to negation and nihilism. Thus Jews, Christians, and others must challenge every aspect of their traditions that overtly or covertly degrades others or nurtures hatred and thus reduces solidarity. If this means confrontation with the divine sources of the religion (as in the Gospels' anti-Semitic tradition or the secondary status of women in certain biblical categories), then this becomes the religious challenge. If the commandments of God lead to collaboration in genocide or weakening of the capacity to resist it, then God, as it were, must be challenged. This challenge would be testimony for God, whereas acquiescence to degradation would be testimony against God.

Secularization: Pro and Con

When the Rabbis perceived the destruction of the temple to be an orienting event, they concluded that it was revealing a new level of relationship between God and Israel. The Destruction "proved" not that there was no God or that God had rejected Israel as the covenant people but that the Divine, as it were, was withdrawing (in later cabala the term used is *tzimtzum*, or "self-limitation") to allow more room for human agency and maturation. In a world where the Red Sea is split to save Israel, God is manifest (cf. Exod. 14:30–31). In a world where Roman legions triumph and the temple is destroyed, God is hidden. God's redemptive acts are now to come more through human agency. Thus Purim (which occurred after the first temple destruction) became the paradigmatic redemptive event. God's name is not mentioned in the Book of Esther—both the redemption in that book and the human agents involved are flawed—but this deliverance is a confirmation of the divine presence. Indeed the Rabbis see the acceptance of the holiday as a reacceptance of the covenant *on a par with Sinai* (cf. *t. Sabb.* 88a). A fortiori, one must suggest that the same process takes place after the Holocaust. The divine is more hidden, and human activity (= "secular" activity) is the agency of divine intervention. At the heart of this new secularism is a hidden relationship to God's presence in history and a lovingkindness that defies death and evil through the re-creation of the image of God and its ground in history.

To put it another way, *holy secularity* becomes the preferred religious mode. Holy secularity focuses on the re-creation of the image of God and of a society that nurtures this human dignity. How does this differ from the theological-secularization movement of the 1960s? This holy secularity acts out of covenantal faithfulness and community memory, drawing strongly on the resources of liturgy and community for its nurture. A holy secularity also opposes the absolutization of the secular. From the Holocaust, holy secularists learn that the humans who claim to be absolute create Auschwitz—a hell to outdo hell. Human becomes God (or absolute) becomes devil or, more accurately, becomes Moloch, that is, idol. One may argue that it was precisely the cutting off of the grounding in the sacred that allowed the affirmations of human power and will of modern culture to metastasize into totalitarian, totally immanent systems. Thus we need a dialectical secularization, one that attacks the full adequacy, even as it affirms the centrality, of the secular. This also challenges all attempts at reversion to pre-Holocaust religious triumphalism, or to religious formalism as substitute for ethics. By this view, all unqualified proclamations of God's authority or God's saving power are inauthentic after the Holocaust.

The sum of these changes is a basic reorientation of the methodology and conceptual approaches of religious Jews and Christians as well as of modernists in general. These changes confirm that the Holocaust is in fact an orienting event. It constitutes (as, I believe, the rebirth of the state of Israel does) the renewed presence of revelation in our times.

The Unfolding of the Covenant, or New Revelation

At the heart of Judaism and Christianity is a covenant of redemption committed to a final unification of history and the divine ideal reality. Later events along the way to the perfection can unfold the meaning of this covenant.

Jeremiah even spoke of a later redemptive event so great that people would speak of the God who brought Israel back to the land rather than the God who took Israel out of Egypt (Jer. 14:14–15; 23:7–8).

Christianity has been tempted by its resurrection theology to claim that now that Christ has come and the redemption has already taken place, as a religion, it is beyond history. Still, the logic of its teaching of a Second Coming makes it come down on the side of a final redemption in history as well. This perforce must leave it open to later events which reveal and illuminate the initial orienting events.

Implicit in the biblical model is an unfolding covenantal relationship between the human and the divine. After the flood, God renounces future use of that weapon to punish sinful humanity (Gen. 8:21-22; 9:9-17) as part of a covenant with Noah. In effect, God is accepting limits in the relationship with humanity out of respect for its freedom. While the Bible places great stress on the divine rewards and punishments for obedience to the later Israelite covenant, there is some movement beyond a simple covenant reward/punishment model after the first destruction of the temple.

After the destruction of the second temple and the crucifixion of Jesus, the Rabbis and the Christians both took the biblical covenantal model to new levels of meaning in their respective religions. Jesus' coming had convinced Christians that a decisive new step of the covenant was unfolding—eventually, this led to the claim that the Old Covenant was superseded. The meanings, rituals, institutions—the way of the New Covenant—were understood as the illumination of the meaning and the reorientation of the Old Covenant in light of Jesus' life and death. In playing out the implications of the covenantal model against the backdrop of the belief that God had become flesh to broaden the covenant and open it to other peoples, Christianity enshrined the *biblical* covenantal model —that is, the model of the God overtly intervening in human affairs to bring salvation—in its theology and liturgy. Overall, the biblical model of divine intervention climaxes in the Christian image of God—in the flesh—intervening to overthrow the facticity of present reality and reveal the true way to redemption. The model of an unmistakably divine Jesus was used in understanding the New Testament passages describing his life. "Defeat" of the divine (that is, Jesus' crucifixion) was obviously impossible since the divine by definition cannot be defeated by humans. Therefore, the defeat was interpreted as "façade." It was a voluntarily chosen fate designed to teach that true victory is the renunciation of power, and winning by the model of suffering love. Winning will be achieved when humanity voluntarily is overcome by this model and wins the same kind of victory over hatred and enemies. By the same token, the message of the Crucifixion could be applied to explain the ongoing unredeemed nature of sociopolitical reality. The answer is that salvation is outside of history, which is the realm where carnal power rules—"The kingdom of God is within you." The alternate answer is that when spiritual salvation triumphs, then as a byproduct the realm of human relationships and society will also be perfected. Either way, the biblical model of manifest divine intervention is enshrined in the life of Jesus and in its centrality in Christian liturgy and self-understanding. To this day, the tendency to evoke "biblical" proofs of Jesus—that is, miracles, earthly rewards, and punishments for faith, and the divine presence found overtly in life—is stronger in Christianity than in Judaism. (Obviously, there is a wide range of views on this matter within each faith, especially because of the impact of modernity, which stimulated tendencies in Christianity to secularize or modify the overt presence of Christ as it led to similar modifications of the concept of God in the parallel Jewish denominational settings.) The reason for the greater Christian emphasis on manifest divine presence is that at the very moment that Christianity was encapsulating an overt divine intervention in history at the heart of its faith testimony, Judaism was unfolding the biblical covenant model in a different direction.

After the destruction of the second temple, the Rabbis had to face the question whether the covenant was over. Had God repudiated the original covenant with Israel? (This is what Christians later concluded.) Was there no God? Was there no more access to God unless the old main channel (the temple) would be rebuilt? The Rabbis ultimately concluded that the covenant was still valid but that Israel was called to a new level of relationship with God. God was more hidden now; God was using great self-control and allowing humanity—even the evil ones—freedom of action. God was more hidden, but humans—the Jews in particular—were called to seek God out.

This interpretation had a profound effect on the operation of the covenant. Although a covenant, by definition, has two partners, in the Bible God is the senior partner, initiating, instructing, rewarding, enforcing. Now the human—incarnated in the people, Israel—became much more of a true partner in the covenant. Indeed the terms "partner" (*shutta*) and "partnership" (*shutfut*) appear repeatedly in rabbinical literature but are never used in the Bible. This human maturation and divine self-limitation has many institutional consequences. A hidden God no longer uses prophets to send direct instructions to the faithful. Thus the Rabbis concluded that prophecy had ended (*t. B. Bat.* 1a). One need not listen to a *bat kol,* a divine voice, in making legal decisions. (Cf. *t. B. Meṣ.* 59a, b.) Note that this is an unfolding of the covenant model in light of the later event and not a repudiation of the earlier model. In the words of the Rabbis, Moses received the Torah at Sinai, handed it over to Joshua, and so on to the prophets, and the prophets handed it over to the men of the Great Assembly (perceived by the Rabbis as the initiators of the rabbinate—(*t. Pirkei 'Abot,* chap. 1, m. 1). The prophetic messenger with divine word is appropriate to a universe where God manifestly intervenes. The Rabbis who use their best judgment based on past models (precedents) of God's activity and instructions are the appropriate channel of communication with the divine when God is hidden. Similarly, in a world of overt divine presence, there are special holy places where the Divine, as it were, is more palpable Presence. After the Destruction, the new holy divine meeting place—the synagogue—could be located all over the world. Significantly, the levels of ritual purity expected there are considerably lower than the temple's. Even prayer bespeaks a more secular setting. Since God speaks much less, humans initiate dialogue and bring their concerns to God. Prayer is really predicated on a divine silence!

The Rabbis suggest that the covenant itself is readopted out of a more hidden (secular) divine redemptive act—Purim—because the Sinai encounter was too overt, too coercive to be appropriate in the new setting. This entire unfolding of the covenant is built on a pedagogical model. God is the teacher; study of Torah is the basic human responsibility; internalization of norms and knowledge is the goal, and education is set up for the masses so that they too can become true partners in the practice and creation of Torah.

One must qualify the description above by the fact that the Rabbis did not consistently secularize. They do incorporate miracle working and concepts of covenantal rewards and punishments into their thinking. Yet the very structure of assumptions and methods shows a significant secularization—and, paradoxically, broadening out—of the divine presence. Thus we can say that Christianity is an unfolding of the biblical covenant initiated by a redemptive event (Jesus' resurrection) which is seen as revelatory. It "fulfills" the Old and moves it into the New Covenant. Rabbinical Judaism is an unfolding of the covenant which is stimulated by a destructive event which is interpreted as calling the human to a new level of relationship to the Divine. Despite the rabbinical denigration of their generations compared to the earlier ones, the fact is that the human attains new maturity, authority, and responsibility in Judaism. By contrast, in Christianity the Divine takes over an even more dominant role (hence the salience of concepts of grace in Christianity over against the significant shrinkage of its role in rabbinical tradition compared to biblical norms). Similarly, the sacramental dimensions of Judaism found in aspects of the temple service are vestigial in rabbinical Judaism but are central in Catholicism.

We can say that for the first two millenniums of their relationship, Judaism functioned in the theological parameters of the rabbinical "partnership," or second stage of the covenant, while Christianity was closer to the unreconstructed biblical world of overt divine presence and intervention. Now the Holocaust is another major event of destruction. Again Jews have had to answer the question whether this event refuted the covenantal faith. Richard Rubenstein has concluded that it has. I would suggest that the bulk of the Jewish people has concluded otherwise. By its behavior, it has upheld the covenant. This includes re-creating the state of Israel and reaffirming Jewish life and culture.

It would appear that Judaism is entering another major phase of the unfolding of the covenant. The hiddenness of God is even deeper, but the shattering of the secular paradigm, as we have seen, suggests that the covenantal responsibility level is being raised again. One might argue that ultimately it is intrinsic in a love/pedagogical model of the covenant that the human partner come of age. To make this possible, the divine partner must self-limit to the point of not intervening to coerce or punish. This is the operative assumption even of most religious Jews in the post-Holocaust Jewish situation.

There are further implications in the unfolding of the covenant.

ple were too "sacramental" and overt
so the rabbinate and synagogue may
Holocaust era. The covenant will be
; the "silent" partner, present, sharing
entially calling on the human to take
e of humanity and for the coming (or
owever, this will be a *called* human
"what doth the Lord require of thee"
secularized speakers—perhaps writers,
s. Paradoxically again, the seculariza-
ness of God's presence from the more
limited number of ...ttings to an almost universal presence;
that is, secular settings will be the focus of religious activity. Prayer
will be expressed in actions and/or will be the prayer of the strong;
that is, it will be silent, less pleading, less repetitious and flattering
to the Divine.

The theological construct that most closely approximates this
description would be that this will be the age of a voluntary covenant. From a conceptual viewpoint, the divine right to command is
forfeit in the Holocaust. Indeed, Roy Eckardt suggested that in light
of the extraordinary suffering which responsibility for the covenant
has brought on Israel and in light of the divine failure to protect
the Jews, God must surely repent of the covenant, that is, plead
guilty by inflicting such exposure to hatred and death on God's
people. Elie Wiesel has spoken of the covenant being broken by
the divine failure to protect the people Israel. I believe that the
Jewish people reacted to this new state by voluntarily reembracing
the covenant. This is expressed in the decisions both to have children and to go on living as Jews. There actually has been an
enormous expansion of Jewish commitment and living in America
in the past three decades. However, the central Jewish response
was to re-create the major biblical symbol and guarantor of the
validity of the covenant, that is, Jewish sovereign presence in and
possession of the land of Israel. Israel is the great statement of life
and redemption of the Jewish people—a response to an unprece-
dented act of destruction—a statement of hope and abiding faith
that there is still a future for redeeming the world.

The implications of a voluntary covenant are many. It offers a theological base for a true pluralism of commitment. Imposed covenants can have one decisive standard. Voluntary covenants can by definition be pluralist and multiform. The central symbol of the involuntary covenant was circumcision—obviously a male-oriented symbol. The additional symbol of a voluntary covenant is likely to be a revived version of the covenant of passing "between the pieces" (*brit bayn habetarim*). Passing between the pieces symbolizes the unification of the ideal and the real—the present reality and the final redemption—which are only a fragment if they split apart. This symbol can be participated in equally by men and women. This new stage opens the door to a new equality—although not necessarily identity—of roles. This equality is demanded by the need for unqualified testimony to the fullness of the divine image and is implied in the identity of fate and of struggle of men and women in the Holocaust. Thus this orienting event calls on believers to reorient—not to repudiate the past models but to move into the new levels of relationship. The call for religious equality of women is not an attack on past halachic models. It is an attempt to raise them to a new level of full human responsibility and religious testimony.

The new state of the covenant suggests that Jews will play a more active role in creating Torah and in bringing the redemption. At the least, new holy days of mourning the destruction (*Yom Ha Shoah,* Holocaust Remembrance Day) and of celebrating the redemption (*Yom Ha Atzmaut,* Israeli Independence Day, and *Yom Yerushalayim,* Jerusalem Liberation Day) will become pillars of the sacred round of covenantal life. (Note that these days qualify for the new stage by being secular—on the surface.)

Many other applications of the orienting event are probable: in the area of ethics (Remember you were hungry in Auschwitz; therefore feed the hungry); in the area of ritual (missions as pilgrimages to Israel, the site of redemption; or to Auschwitz, the site of the destruction; eating potato peels in memory of Bergen Belsen). A new secular Bible telling the story of the great catastrophe and great redemption or a Talmud exploring the laws and ways of the new state of sovereignty and/or power may well emerge. By definition, such books will pass for secular but will be the sacred Scriptures of this new era of revelation. One may guess that facticity and accuracy will be the hallmarks of the new myth's statements. Thus survivors' accounts or ghetto diaries will likely be among the new Scriptures.

Elsewhere I have documented my conviction that the Holocaust will be a major event in Christian history as well.[6] It is clear that Christianity will not be able to overcome its legacy of guilt for the Holocaust without a major purging of its sources of Jew hatred. This will take head-on confrontation with the Gospels' and church fathers' tradition of supersessionism and anti-Semitism. The capacity for major development can come only from recognition that the Holocaust is an orienting event in Christian history. The covenantal model which Christianity incorporates is, by definition, open to further illumination and reorientation.

The Holocaust as an orienting event suggests a more "secular" reading of Jesus' life. It reveals that the process of redemption was less advanced than Christians assumed. This need not take away from the divinity of Jesus' life or its significance as orienting event. It suggests, however, that the life would have been deliberately lived so as to be, in its visible form, relatively indistinguishable from that of other teachers and would-be redeemers. Similarly, the Resurrection may barely have happened, that is, would be subject to interpretation as a natural event or as not having happened. For example, initially an empty tomb is found. An evocative rather than manifest nature is more appropriate a revelation in light of the Holocaust. Contrary to Christian polemics, this hiddenness need not be interpreted as designed to trap Jews in their willful stubbornness—a stubbornness which appears all the more glaring when the image of Jesus' life is manifestly divine. Rather it was meant to evoke differential response—positive from the founders of Christianity; negative from the Jews, who were called to remain faithful to their covenant. The reconstruction of the gospel message and the sense of human responsibility implied in the Holocaust suggests a major turn in Christianity—at the least, it would enter its "rabbinical" era. This presages a major new emphasis on worldly redemption, personal responsibility, and human cocreativity in Christianity. What new institutions and leadership it will develop remain to be seen. Christianity would be both absolute yet nonimperialistic, one that could embrace the world without losing its soul.

I believe that Jews would respond to such a Christianity with an acceptance that goes beyond tolerance and/or tactical pluralism. They would recognize the indigenous nature of a Messianic development, the authenticity of a Christian responsibility-taking that seeks to realize the ends of the covenant. They would acknowledge the legitimacy of an unfolding that does not destroy or deny the unfailing—indeed, the equally unfolding—life of the Jewish covenant.

The question is, will Christianity rather cling to its insistence on the finality of Christ's revelation and thereby be guilty of the very hardheartedness it falsely charged Judaism with in the early centuries? The task of faithful believers is not to rule out further illumination but to respond gratefully to any orienting event that sheds light on the tactics, the goal, and the way. If Christianity responds, the coming of the next millennium may be more millennial than current modernist complacency expects. The unfolding of the covenant and its realization are in our hands.

Notes

1. Henry L. Feingold, "Determining the Uniqueness of the Holocaust: The Factor of Historical Values," *SHOAH* 2, no. 2 (Spring 1981): 5.

2. Cf. Elie Wiesel, *Legends of Our Time* (New York, 1970), p. 176; Alexander Donat, *The Holocaust Kingdom: A Memoir* (New York, 1978), p. 103: "We fell victim to our faith in mankind . . ."

3. Primo Levi, *Survival in Auschwitz* (New York, 1971), p. 82.

4. See Helen Fein, *Accounting for Genocide* (New York, 1979).

5. See, on all this, Irving Greenberg, "Cloud of Smoke, Pillar of Fire: Judaism, Christianity and Modernity After the Holocaust," in *Auschwitz: Beginning of a New Era?*, ed. Eva Fleischner (New York, 1977).

6. See Irving Greenberg, "New Revelations and New Patterns in the Relationship of Judaism and Christianity," *Journal of Ecumenical Studies* 16, no. 2 (Spring 1979): 249–67.

Religious Values After the Holocaust: A Catholic View

DAVID TRACY

Catholic Theology

The expression *Catholic theology* means, of course, the self-interpretation of the Catholic Christian religious tradition. And yet this seemingly obvious description of the task of Catholic theology needs further explanation. Only then can we hope to clarify the explicitly theological task of Catholic Christianity in relation to that event of sheer negativity we hesitatingly call the Holocaust— an event which, with Arthur Cohen, we might more fittingly name theologically the *tremendum* of our age.[1]

To assume that Catholic theologians practice Catholic theology by engaging in the self-interpretation of the Catholic tradition is, in fact, to imply several factors needing explication. First, the principal task of the theologian is one of interpretation of both the tradition and the contemporary situation. Theology is a task, therefore, for finite, historical interpreters living in a particular cultural situation and attempting to render fitting interpretations of their religious tradition for and in that situation.[2]

Second, theologians as interpreters in this case are also, by definition, those who in some recognizable manner participate in that religious tradition. Thereby do theologians commit themselves to appropriate the tradition's own authoritative norms (its classics) as guides to interpretation.

Third, in the case of Catholic theology, this appropriation is likely to stress the need for taking account of the classics of the whole tradition from the original apostolic witnesses in the New Testament to the present experience of the entire church community, as well as (in the language of the Second Vatican Council) the "signs of the times" in one's own age. It is also the case historically that Catholic theologians have tended to emphasize the trustworthiness of the whole tradition (usually under the rubric of "the development of doctrine"). Catholics have generally, therefore, emphasized interpretation as a hermeneutics of retrieval of the resources of the tradition for the present. In recent years, however, another mode of interpretation has come to play a more and more central role in Catholic theology. This second kind of interpretation can be called a hermeneutics of suspicion upon the possible errors, illusions, and distortions that may also be present in so long, so rich, so complex, and so ambiguous a tradition as that of Catholic Christianity.[3]

In terms of our historical experience, it hardly seems necessary to recall that every tradition, including every religious tradition, is properly described as ambiguous in its reality. For any particular participant in a religious tradition, therefore, two realities will operate: First, a fundamental trust in the disclosive and transformative religious realities of the tradition. That trust and loyalty are named faith. Faith's self-interpretation is called theology. Second, a recognition that alongside fundamental trust in and loyalty to the tradition lies a suspicion upon the possible presence of errors, illusions, distortions in the tradition itself.

Yet my appeal to the need for a Catholic hermeneutics of suspicion, based on a recognition of ambiguities in the tradition alongside (not replacing) a hermeneutics of retrieval based on a fundamental trust in the tradition, is not simply an appeal to our contemporary experience. Rather the familiar appeal in Catholic theology to the *theological* need to "discern the signs of the time" is only the first indication of this demand for suspicion. The traditional Catholic themes of *ecclesia semper reformanda* ("the church always in need of reform") and the theme, well formulated by Catholic theologians from Augustine to Rahner, of the theological reality of a "sinful church" (not only a "church of sinners"), alongside the theological understanding of church as eschatological sacrament of Christ and world, already indicate the need for a Catholic hermeneutics of suspicion. Sin, after all, is a far more radical charge than error, illusion, distortion in our earlier formulation.

Moreover, as the Catholic-Protestant polemics of the past fade into unmourned memory, it becomes clear that the reformatory principle has become a major moment in Catholic theology itself. As Paul Tillich stated years ago on the Protestant side, Reformation theology needs to appropriate "Catholic substance" along with its "Protestant principle." As one should also add, Catholic theology needs to appropriate far more than it often does that Protestant principle as part of its own Catholic Christian substance. As both Catholic and Protestant theologians, moreover, have entered into serious dialogue with Jewish theologians, both Catholics and Protestants have learned anew how Jewish a religion Christianity finally is. Above all, they have learned that the Jewish prophetic, the self-critical, self-reformatory, both suspicious and retrieving eschatological reality of our own Christian and Jewish authoritative biblical faith must be more fully retrieved.

To retrieve those prophetic and eschatological Jewish strains in Christianity is to demand that a major part of contemporary Christian theological interpretation should be a hermeneutics of suspicion upon the actual realities of the religious tradition, a tradition recognized *theologically* as fundamentally trustworthy yet also recognized theologically as ambiguous and demanding constant prophetic self-reform. The route from the anti-Judaic statements of the New Testament through the revolting anti-Jewish polemics of John Chrysostom and others in the patristic period through the explicit (and yet more deadly, the implicit) "teaching of contempt" tradition in the Christian tradition to the virulent, revolting anti-Semitism that can pervade and clearly has pervaded many a Christian unconscious are merely the most obvious examples of the radical ambiguities within the Christian religious tradition.

As the prophetic strain is religiously appropriated and theologically employed in contemporary Catholic theology, moreover, the disclosures—both painful and necessary—of further ambiguities in the very tradition which Catholics fundamentally trust and to which they remain loyal increase. The attempts to reform church struc-

tures in the prophetically oriented theologies of Küng and Schille-
beeckx, for example, are grounded in a profound faith and trust
in the tradition's own norm, Jesus Christ, as these theologians attempt to free the "dangerous" prophetic memory of Jesus upon the
actualities of present church life. The attempts to disclose the repressed ideologies of sexism, classism, oppression, and alienation in
traditional and modern Christian life and thought by the Third
World liberation theologians, the black theologians, and the femi-
nist theologians are *theologically* grounded in this biblical prophetic
strain in Christianity itself. The liberation theologians seek to release the half-forgotten, often repressed memory of the suffering of
the oppressed—those who are special, privileged to God, from the
great prophets to Jesus. They release this prophetic hermeneutics
of suspicion in order to charge the church to be faithful to its own
possibility and command. Those Catholic theologians who have
exposed the ideological distortions of anti-Judaism and anti-
Semitism in the tradition—such theologians as Flannery, Ruether,
Baum, and Pawlikowski—live in and by that prophetic demand,
that inner-Catholic demand for the religious reality of constant
self-criticism and self-reform. They live in and by the theological
reality of both retrieval and suspicion. It is crucial to see that all
these Catholic theologians are as deeply engaged in a hermeneutics
of retrieval of the tradition as their curiously untroubled colleagues.
Yet what these theologians see is precisely that really to retrieve the
prophetic, eschatological strain which empowers Christianity as a
religion is also to retrieve the theological necessity for a hermeneutics of suspicion upon the radical ambiguities of the tradition—the
whole tradition from its beginnings to the present. No less than
more "traditional" Catholic theologies of retrieval are these theologies of both retrieval and suspicion (indeed, often retrievals of the
prophetic strain itself through its release of religious suspicions
upon the ideological distortions in the tradition) grounded in
Catholic faith. That faith bears all the marks of authentic faith: a
fundamental trust and loyalty to the tradition mediating the dangerous memory of Jesus, the prophetic memory of the suffering of
the oppressed, and the hope released by the proleptic eschatological
event of the ministry-death-resurrection of Jesus Christ.

My original description of the task of Catholic theology, therefore, as "the self-interpretation of the Catholic religious tradition" must yield to the fuller description suggested by these theological remarks. Involved in the self-interpretation of the tradition, the systematic theologian as a participating member of the tradition will be grounded in a fundamental trust and loyalty to the tradition itself and will be engaged, therefore, in a fundamental hermeneutics of retrieval of the tradition's own founding, classic, authoritative resources. As thus grounded, the theologian must also retrieve the prophetic strain empowering the whole tradition. Thereby must the theologian engage in a hermeneutics of suspicion as well— suspicion upon, in, and for the sake of the tradition itself. Like any interpreter of any cultural or religious tradition, the theological interpreter remains a radically finite, historical being. Like any finite, historical persons, theologians as well remain rooted in their own ambiguities: attempting to provide critical reflections and appropriate interpretations for and in the tradition; recognizing that each of us bears a personal and cultural history that both frees and binds us; recognizing that not only finitude and historicity but error, illusion, distortion, and even sin are as much a part of the theologian's actuality as of anyone else's; recognizing, therefore, that no theologian can claim to speak for the whole church but that each must attempt to develop interpretative proposals for the church. Those proposals can be grounded in a fundamental trust and loyalty yet formulated hermeneutically as both retrieval and suspicion. To attempt more is to deny the radical historicity of every theological interpreter. To attempt less is to deny the risk that every theological interpretation must be.

For these reasons, like some other Catholic theologians, I have formulated the task of the theologian in the following terms: the attempt to develop mutually critical correlations between interpretations of the tradition and our contemporary experience. Such, for myself, is the principal interpretative task of every theology. Such, on the tradition's own terms (its demand to discern the signs of the times, to engage in prophetic discernment) is the demand and the risk imposed upon every theology.

I have spoken so far of the Catholic theologian's relationship to the tradition. I have argued that the tradition itself demands that our contemporary experience operate in the appropriation and interpretation of the tradition. It is time, however, to shift the focus to that contemporary experience, more exactly to that overwhelming "sign" of our times we call the Holocaust, to see what differences that event might make for the reinterpretation of the Catholic tradition.

The Holocaust and Catholic Theology

I understand the historical event called the Holocaust as an event of sheer, unmitigated negativity: an event disclosing an evil that is incommensurable, incomprehensible—indeed, as Fackenheim, Cohen, Greenberg, and others have persuasively argued, a unique event.[4] Arthur Cohen's expression for that event—the *tremendum*— seems to me to capture the religious and theological dimensions of the event itself. The event is tremendous in the original meaning of that word—earthshaking and frightening. The event is tremendous in the religious meaning of the word—awesome, incomprehensible, frightening, and world shattering. The Holocaust, in Catholic theological terms, discloses the classic countersign of our age. That negative countersign changes the optimistic, secure, consoling signs of the times in our age into signs of radical ambiguity. How can we simply praise what the theological tradition calls the world when the world produced this? How can we simply stand by and continue optimistic theologies of the world when we recall that our Western humanist world either collapsed in the face of that vile destruction of all traditional Greek, Latin, and German humanist cultural values and traditions or else stood by and did little or nothing to stop the horror? How can we stand by and continue to develop theologies of the church and the tradition as if the Holocaust did not happen? How can we do so, as Christians, when we recall that the Christian churches, both Protestant and Catholic, stood by, watched, and did little or nothing to stop the *tremendum.* That individual Christians and individual humanists heard that call and acted, suffered, and died can give the rest of us some heart that the ideals of those traditions did live even then. But that the official churches or whole groups of church congregations did little or nothing in the face of that reality is a fact which commands profound religious repentance and demands genuine theological response.

I submit that the Holocaust is the classic negative event of our age, an event that bears the religious dimension of the *tremendum*; an event that does not displace the founding religious events of either Judaism or Christianity; yet an event that demands the release, for Christians, of a profound Christian hermeneutics of suspicion upon many traditional interpretations of the Christian tradition. Through the work of the theologians mentioned above, that hermeneutical task, that painful and necessary theological task, has already begun. Through the person of Pope John XXIII after his encounter with Jules Isaac, through the recent statements of the French and Dutch bishops, that task has already begun in the official church. But it would be dishonest to state anything more than that the task has begun. If one can infer from the silence of most theologians the fact that they still stand back and refuse to face this *tremendum*, we must conclude that for many theologians and many Christians, the painful, necessary disclosures of unrelieved evil of the Holocaust have not been allowed to touch their interpretations of either the world or the Christian tradition.

The fact remains, however, that the hermeneutics of suspicion released by the Holocaust can and should become for Christians a demand for a Christian theological hermeneutics of suspicion upon both tradition and world. In the light of that suspicion, we may yet find the possibilities for new hermeneutics of retrieval of half-forgotten or even repressed aspects of the Christian tradition.

Allow me to give some examples of both the suspicions raised by the Holocaust and the possibilities of retrieval of sometimes forgotten aspects of the tradition which the reality of the Holocaust does disclose. I will concentrate my major attention on the fundamental doctrines of salvation, Christ, and God. Before those more controversial aspects of my proposal, however, allow me to note some prior issues that demand further and continuous reflection.

The first factor is the most obvious and perhaps the most deadly: Christianity has explicitly allowed in the writings of some of its most cherished fathers of the faith (Saint John Crysostom being only the most famous example) a long teaching of contempt for the Jews and for the Jewish religion. Christianity has implicitly allowed more popular expressions of this contempt to perdure even in its catechisms and its popular piety. The liturgical reforms of the Good Friday service initiated by Pope John XXIII and the catechetical reforms initiated since Vatican II are merely the first expressions of the suspicions that must be cast on this revolting tradition of both implicit and explicit teachings of contempt. Every vestige of that tradition should not only be removed but repented for. Repentance and reformatory action alone are worthy of a tradition that honors the prophetic spirit now released upon the tradition's own sins—sins, to recall the traditional Catholic vocabulary, of both omission and commission. The story told by Edward Flannery in *The Anguish of the Jews,* as well as the histories of the church during the Nazi period, calls not only for reform (as almost all admit) but for profound and meaningful repentance—as some official church leaders (notably the Dutch and French bishops) now insist.

Moreover, the painful, repressed memories of Christian anti-Semitism have also been aided by the anti-Judaic statements of the New Testament, especially but not solely in the Gospel of John. If those scriptural statements cannot be excised, then minimally they should always be commented upon whenever used in liturgical settings and noted critically in every Christian commentary on the Scriptures. The history of the effects of those New Testament anti-Judaic outbursts should signal the need for Christians, singly and communally, to reflect upon ways to banish forever this bad side of the good news of the New Testament. Those anti-Judaic statements of the New Testament bear *no* authoritative status for Christianity. Even the most "fulfillment"-oriented Christology has no real theological need for them. The heart of the New Testament message—the love who is God—should release the demythologizing power of its own prophetic meaning to rid the New Testament and Christianity once and for all of all these statements.

To release a Christian hermeneutics of suspicion, I suggested earlier, can also release a Christian heremeneutics of retrieval. These first examples of suspicion, in fact, also suggest the necessity of retrieval. In a real sense, this has begun to occur powerfully among Christian theologians—that is, among all those (I include here the liberation theologians) who have begun to recognize the profoundly Jewish character of Christianity itself. The Christian God is none other than the God of Israel, the God of Abraham, Isaac, and Jacob. Our Christ is none other than Jesus the Jew of Nazareth. Our sacred texts are none other than the Hebrew Scriptures, which also serve as our Old Testament, and the apostolic writings—the apostolic writings of the early Jewish Christians, which we call the New Testament.

Yet to retrieve the Jewishness of Christianity is also to retrieve the possibility of recalling, on Christian grounds, that for the Christian the Jews are and will remain God's chosen people. The Christian as Christian can and, I believe, must affirm that chosenness of the Jews as a theological reality. The contemporary Christian can do so, I also believe, without the ambiguities, if not incoherence, in Paul's real but confusing affirmation of that chosenness. The earlier attempts to revive the notion of two covenants of Hans Urs von Balthasar and Jacques Maritain on the Catholic side of the dialogue and the extraordinary theological position of Franz Rosenzweig on the Jewish side indicate that this aspect of the Pauline notion can perhaps be retrieved without Paul's own ambiguities. At any rate, these noble theological developments of Rosenzweig, von Balthasar, Maritain, and others already indicate that every Catholic (even such relatively conservative Catholics as Maritain and von Balthasar) can and should affirm, on inner Catholic grounds, that the Jews were, are, and will remain God's chosen, covenanted people. Entailed by this theological commitment are others. Catholics should learn the history of the Hebrew Scriptures not only through the Christian eyes of the New Testament and Christian Old Testament scholars but through the eyes of Jewish scholars as well; Catholics should learn—which means practically that Catholic institutions, especially colleges and seminaries, should teach—the history of postbiblical Judaism. When we learn, for example, more about the rabbinical teaching, we will be unlikely to repeat the poisonous clichés in the law that still inflict Christian biblical scholarship and theology (especially, as E. P. Sanders has persuasively shown,[5] Pauline scholarship).

A second theological issue relates to the first. In terms of my rubric of the hermeneutics of suspicion released by the Holocaust upon the tradition, the issue can be formulated as the nature of Christian salvation in the world. Insofar as one kind of Catholic spirituality is spiritualizing (or unworldly) and privatizing (or nonpublic) and insofar as that spirituality aided individual Christians to avoid their historical responsibilities in the situation of the Holocaust, contemporary Catholic theological reflection on salvation and spirituality needs to become yet more suspicious of all nonworldly, nonpolitical forms of spirituality. It should be added, of course, that at least since the document *Gaudium et Spes* at Vatican II (and the prior work of theologians like Teilhard de Chardin), any unworldly and surely private spirituality has already been under Catholic theological suspicion.

And yet it is clearly not the case, in the perspective of the Holocaust, that the proposed solutions of Teilhard or other incarnationalist and Christian humanist theologians or even the optimistic appraisal of the world in *Gaudium et Spes* (or, it might be added, the too optimistic appraisal of secularity in my own *Blessed Rage for Order* and in similar 'secular' theologies) can any longer suffice. For the suspicions released by the Holocaust are radical suspicions not only upon unworldly and privatizing spiritualities. They also cast suspicion upon the this-worldly and antiprivatizing spiritualities which accord too optimistic a portrait of the world.

In that sense, theological reflection upon the Holocaust reinforces and indeed, as we shall see below, radicalizes the kind of Catholic liberation and political theological appraisal of the systematic distortions present not only in the church tradition but in the secular, worldly tradition as well. This point is worth dwelling upon. For in the present neoconservative resurgence in both Catholicism and the wider culture, the exposé of the radical ambiguity of the world and the secular can often become an occasion (and sometimes an excuse) to return to a purely spiritual, unworldly, and finally private spirituality. The latter cases range from a retrieval of the *fuga mundi* tradition of an earlier asceticism through the temptations (not necessity) of charismatic renewals to the more moderate, but no less deadly, retreats from the world of neoconservative theologians.

Just as George Steiner's profound critique of Western humanism in the light of the Holocaust or the Frankfurt school's analysis of the dialectic of the Enlightenment suggest for secular culture, theological analyses of the profound distortions revealed in the world and secular culture should not become the occasion to retreat from a spirituality for and in the world. The example of Catholic liberation and political theologies is instructive here. For these theological critiques from the Left do disclose through their analyses of the classism, racism, sexism, anti-Semitism, oppression, and alienation present in both church traditions and secular traditions that any theological account of the radical ambiguity of the world cannot occur without a radical affirmation of the world. In theological terms, we are freed *from* the world *for* the world. The violence of this language (freed from) is exact and does cast profound suspicion on any optimistic appraisal of the world. But we are freed from the world for the world. To ignore that "freedom for" is to risk developing spiritualities and theologies of salvation which will betray the retrieval of the worldly, historical, political character of the central biblical and traditional understandings of salvation in the world. In short, the Holocaust piercingly casts a radical hermeneutics of suspicion upon any optimistic theological appraisals of the world. That event also casts a suspicion upon any pessimistic spiritualities of retreat from our historical and political responsibility.

The Catholic "return to history and the world" initiated by Vatican II has received its proper corrective from those political and liberation theologians. For these theologians have developed profound theological hermeneutics of suspicion upon the world and an equally profound hermeneutics of retrieval of the this-worldly reality of Christian salvation. They have retrieved half-forgotten (and, it should be noted, almost always Jewish rather than Greek) resources of the tradition. The recent theology of the Catholic political theologian Johann Baptist Metz is instructive here.[6] Metz has attempted to retrieve the apocalyptic tradition insofar as apocalyptic both negates all complacency in contemporary history and at the same time demands action in and for the world in that same history. Metz has appealed as well to the profoundly Jewish theological sensibilities of Walter Benjamin's retrieval of eschatological narratives. Narrative—a traditional form of Jewish but rarely Christian theology—is retrievable precisely in

97

Benjamin's sense: keeping alive the prophetic memory of the suffering of the oppressed. Moreover, the appeal of Latin American liberation theologians that the New Testament can be read properly only in the light of the this-worldly and historical character of the Jewish notion of redemption is yet another sign that in our post-Holocaust age the suspicions released on any optimistic appraisal of the world can become further retrievals (if often unconscious ones) of the Jewish, this-worldly, ethical, and historical side of Christian salvation itself.

I suggested above that the event of the Holocaust has released a hermeneutics of suspicion that reinforces the suspicions of the liberation and political theologians on the world. At the same time, the Holocaust radicalizes those suspicions and those possibilities of retrieval. This point is important to note theologically for, with the notable exceptions of Baum and Ruether, Catholic liberation and political theologians have not yet noted the radicalization of the more usual liberation suspicions upon the world that the event of the Holocaust demands. In short, the Latin American theologians as well as the Euro-American political theologians have generally not allowed the profound suspicions released by the Holocaust upon traditional christological formulations to inform their perspective. Rather, in spite of their radical critique of traditional and modern liberal theologies of salvation, these theologians formulate their Christologies with a seemingly untroubled use of such biblical and traditional categories as the New Covenant, fulfillment, and the law-gospel contrast. And yet the question must be raised—as Baum, Pawlikowski, and Ruether have properly raised it for Catholic theology—whether so untroubled a retrieval of traditional christological language can be any more countenanced than an untroubled use of traditional salvation language.

For myself, the suspicion which the Holocaust discloses for traditional christological language is this: does the fundamental Christian belief in the ministry, death, and resurrection of Jesus Christ demand a Christology that either states or implies that Judaism has been displaced by Christianity? As we saw above, Franz Rosenzweig gave one famous suggestion on how both Christianity and Judaism can be recognized as two covenants from the viewpoint of Judaism. Hans Urs von Balthasar and Jacques Maritain made analogous suggestions from the Catholic side. In a post-Holocaust situation, however, it does become questionable whether the history of the effects of Christian theological fulfillment language or law-gospel language or even the New Covenant language can really be retrieved without seeming to imply that God's covenant with the chosen people, the Jews, is abrogated and that Judaism becomes, in the new covenantal Christian perspective, a spent religion.

Clearly the intent of New Covenant language need not imply the latter and does not for von Balthasar, Maritain, and others. Still, the historical effects of that language, including the effects of Christian caricatures of Judaism as a legalistic religion, the effects of Christian ignorance of postbiblical Judaism in its full richness and complexity, the effects of the easy if often implicit move from fulfillment or New Covenant language to displacement or substitution language should render Christian theologians suspicious even of these noble theologies of retrieval based on a real Jewish-Christian dialogue.

The post-Rosenzweig Jewish "return into history" must be matched, on the Catholic side, with a Catholic return into history. In sum, it is not possible on scriptural grounds to so spiritualize the notion of Messiah that that office loses all relationship to the central Jewish concept of "Messianic times." Any purely realized eschatology (including those informing purely incarnationalist theologies) can maintain itself only at the price of ignoring two central realities: first, the clear presence of the eschatological "not yet" in the New Testament itself, and second, the stark negativity of the radical not yet in our age disclosed in all its horror by the Holocaust.

For Christians to recognize the reality of the negative is to retrieve, theologically, the eschatological reality of the not yet. For Christians to retrieve the reality of the not yet as a historical reality is to recall that the concept Messiah cannot (by being spiritualized) be divorced from the reality of Messianic times. The presence of several Christologies in the New Testament itself (including Christologies where the not yet plays a crucial role, as in Mark's suffering-Messiah christology) demands the following recognition: however influential in later Christian history, theological pure fulfillment models and ahistorical Messiah models are not the only New Testament models that can be employed to express the fundamental Christian belief in the ministry, death, and resurrection of Jesus Christ.

To employ the language of a proleptic Christology seems to me an appropriate route to take. For to affirm the belief in Jesus Christ is, for the Christian, to affirm the faith that in the ministry, death, and resurrection of Jesus the decisive token, manifestation, prolepsis of the future reign of God (and, thereby, of Messianic times) is both already here in a proleptic form (indeed, for myself, has been manifested as always already here) and, just as really, not yet here.

This christological belief—fundamental to Christianity—is a belief that, of course, no Jewish believer can accept. And yet what the Jew can, I believe, recognize in this is that however really this Christian belief divides these two faith communities (as it does), this Christian belief in no way implies the displacement of Judaism by Christianity. Christology thus reformulated as proleptic reaffirms on inner-Christian grounds the status of the Jews as God's chosen, covenanted people. Christology can and should resist the Christian temptation to so spiritualize the notion of Messiah as to wrench it from real history and thereby from the notion of Messianic times. The always/already/not yet structure of belief pervading Israel's covenant with God and Israel's expectancy of Messianic times remains the fundamental always/already/not yet structure of Christian belief as well. Where the two religious communities divide remains as clear as ever. For the Christian, it is in Jesus as the Christ that the prolepsis of those future times is decisively glimpsed. For the Christian, to believe in Jesus as Messiah and Christ is to state the Christian belief in the worthwhileness of the risk of a life of discipleship of this Jesus—a life modeled on the ministry of and words of Jesus. That risk is grounded in the Christian belief in the necessity for action in history and for the world. That action is grounded, for the Christian, in the cross and its disclosure of the reality of suffering for those who will risk that life and in the resurrection and its disclosure of hope for the future—both the future of real history and the future of an afterlife. The individual Christians who took the risk of that model—that *imitatio Christi*—in the struggle for the Jews against the blasphemous and obscene evil of Nazism are those Christians whose lives should remind us that the very life of Christianity endures not by resting in the theologically false security of an ahistorical triumphalist Christology. Christianity lives religiously only by its faith, risk, hope in the always, already, not yet event of the ministry, death, and resurrection of Jesus Christ.

Revisionary suggestions for Christology in a post-Holocaust age similar to that suggested above have already occurred among Catholic theologians. But as far as I am aware, the ultimate theological issue, the understanding of God, has yet to receive much reflection from Catholic theologians. And yet, as Schleiermacher correctly insisted, the doctrine of God can never be "another" doctrine for theology but must pervade all doctrines. Here Jewish theology, in its reflections on the reality of God since the *tremendum* of the Holocaust, has led the way for all serious theological reflection.

I will not presume to comment upon the inner-Jewish theological debate on this central theological issue. I will presume to state, however, that no Christian theologian can afford to ignore that discussion as if it were simply an inner-Jewish theological issue.

Rather, as I have urged throughout these reflections, the event of the Holocaust is at least as much a theological challenge for Christian self-understanding as it is for Jewish. The hermeneutics of suspicion released by the Holocaust upon Christian self-understanding touches, I have suggested, theological interpretations of such central Christian doctrines as the nature of salvation and the doctrine of Christ. Yet for Christian theologians to stop there would, I believe, be to forget that theology is finally and at every moment *theo*-logy. The concentration of Jewish theological reflection on the doctrine of God in the light of the Holocaust must become, for both Jew and Christian, the heart of the theological matter. There is no other God for the Christian than the God of Israel—the God of Abraham, Isaac, Jacob, and Jesus Christ. The Scriptures we share—the Hebrew Scriptures—are an authoritative

source for the reflection upon the reality of God for us both. No
Christian theologian can still feel free to ignore the extraordinary
complexity of those Scriptures' reflection on God—the anger at
God in Lamentations 3, the God of love and justice in Deuter-
onomy and the great prophets, the contrast, if not conflict, in the
portraits of God in Amos, Hosea, and Job. Any Christian theologian who, in this post-Holocaust age, can repeat the specious
claim that the New Testament understanding of God as a God
of love is either radically different from the God of love of Deuter-
onomy or Hosea, or contradicts the God of justice and wrath of
Amos, or eliminates the profound problematic of Job or Lamentations 3 is at best a Marcionite, at worst one who will not face
the sheer negativity of the Holocaust and its painful demand
upon every Christian believer in the God of Abraham, Isaac, Jacob,
and Jesus Christ.

The first step, therefore, for Christian theologians to take in
reflecting upon the reality of God in the light of the Holocaust
is to retrieve, once again, our Jewish roots. We need to retrieve
those roots in such manner that we take with full theological
seriousness the complex portrait of God in the Hebrew Scriptures.
We can also hope that in the light of the reflections of post-
Holocaust Jewish theologians, Christian theologians begin to take
more seriously as well the postbiblical resources of Judaism in its
diverse and complex reflections on the reality of God: from the
subtleties of rabbinical Judaism through the mystical negativity
in God of cabalistic Judaism through the retrieval of mad midrash
in Elie Wiesel and Emil Fackenheim.

Moreover, the very negativity of the event of the Holocaust
forces a suspicion upon many traditional Christian theological
understandings of God which do not seriously take account of
that kind of overwhelming evil. Surely we should suggest that
yet another half-forgotten tradition in Christian theology needs
retrieval after the release of those suspicions: I refer especially
to the so-called negative or apophatic theological traditions. I
refer as well to the recognition and theological appropriation of
different kinds and degrees of negativity in the theological understanding of God: in the radical incomprehensibility tradition of
Aquinas and Rahner, the hidden-revealed God of Luther and

Calvin, God as ground and abyss in Schelling and Tillich, God as absent and present in John of the Cross and Teresa of Avila.

Christian theology, I believe, is just at the beginning of this properly theological reflection on the reality of God. That such reflection is forced upon us is the result of any serious theological reflection upon the Holocaust. Such reflection may also find resources in our common Scriptures with our Jewish colleagues; resources in the reflections of postbiblical Jewish thought as they are now being retrieved by the daring, necessary, painful enterprise of post-Holocaust Jewish theology; resources as well in the negative theologies of Christian theological tradition and in the negativity embedded, if widely overlooked, in such classic Christian theological understandings of God as Pseudo-Dionysius, Aquinas, Luther, Calvin, Hegel, Schelling, Tillich, and Rahner. If we are merely at the beginning of this theological reflection on God, then it becomes imperative to recognize the reality of suspicion and the possibilities of retrieval. I can make no further claim for my own reflections on this ultimate theological question at the present save to state, briefly and tentatively, how that suspicion has affected my own theological understanding of the reality of God.

No more than a heuristic sketch of a direction for thinking of the reality of God after the Holocaust seems possible here. Yet that much, at least, should be attempted. Otherwise we may be tempted to forget that all theological thought is finally the always inadequate and always necessary attempt to understand the God who revealed God's very self to us.

For myself, the question of God in the light of the Holocaust is not principally a question of theodicy. I can understand and respect the posing of questions of theodicy in the classical theological tradition in two primary cases: when the question of natural evil is raised, the question can be posed sharply; when the question of human evil is raised (as in the paradigmatic case of the Holocaust), the classic reflections seem to me to reveal their inadequacy. More exactly, those classic reflections are appropriate as reflections not on genuine, concrete evil but on the condition for the possibility of evil, namely, the divine gift of human freedom which allows the frightening misuses of that freedom in human evil. Indeed, classical philosophical and theological reflections on the nature of evil are usually also transcendental or metaphysical in character—as in the honorable tradition of understanding evil metaphysically (as nonbeing) in Aquinas.

These classic reflections continue to provide real resources for reflection upon metaphysical or transcendental conditions of possibility on the question of God and evil. Yet the Holocaust as a sheer evil perpetrated by human beings on human beings also discloses the real limitations of all such metaphysical or transcendental reflection on conditions of possibility. Rather the overwhelming horror in the historical concreteness of the Holocaust makes us recognize that even if we begin with classic theological reflections on the conditions of possibility of freedom, human evil (as nonbeing), and on God's transcendence and immanence or the divine permissive will, we could not end there. With the tradition, we can recognize after the Holocaust that there is no philosophical solution to the question of evil. Even the classic analyses of the nonbeing of evil indicate, not a solution, but the radicalization of the insight (the inverse insight) that there is no philosophical solution. With the tradition, we can also recognize that any properly theological understanding of God's reality must allow for three factors: philosophical coherence, appropriateness to the scriptural portrait of God, and existential resonance with human beings' concrete experiences of both God and radical evil.

Yet as soon as we mention this last requirement we also recognize the profound question which the Holocaust poses to the religious believer as ultimately a religious, not a philosophical, question. For the religious experience of God as, for example, an immanent-transcendent God of love clashes with the equally religious sense of the mystery of the profound evil disclosed in the *tremendum* of the Holocaust. The appeals to Job, to Lamentations 3, to "mad midrash" and to the suffering servant of Second Isaiah or the crucified God of the Christian symbolism are profoundly religious-theological responses to the issue. Each of these responses challenges either explicitly or implicitly the possibility of a philosophical response. And here, surely, they are correct. For the real conflict we sense in the Holocaust as Jews and Christians is not a philosophical conflict between human freedom and divine transcendence, or between evil as a nonbeing and God's permissive will, but a profoundly religious conflict. That conflict is a sense of being torn apart religiously: by the radically disorienting experience of unmitigated evil in the Holocaust on the one hand and a sustaining experience of God as revealed as a God of pure, unbounded love on the other.

Religiously and theologically considered, therefore, the Holocaust is not primarily a problem of theodicy in the classic mold but a problem of anthropodicy. Yet to say this is not to suggest that there is no rethinking necessary for the doctrine of God in the *tremendum* darkness of the Holocaust. I have argued elsewhere and at length that even before considering the Holocaust, Christian theology should accept a process understanding of God as more coherent, more faithful to the scriptural portrait of God as really affected and affecting human beings (that is, really a God of love) and as more resonant to our contemporary experience of change as a responsible candidate for perfection language and, therefore, for God language. But even this now familiar process theological proposal must itself be rethought and radicalized in a post-Holocaust age.

Even those theologians like myself who continue to believe that process categories are, in fact, more philosophically coherent than classically theistic categories; that they are more appropriate categories for understanding the scriptural affirmation of God as a God of love; and that they are more existentially resonant to our postclassical understanding of change and process as anthropological constants and marks of perfectibility, not imperfection, cannot after the Holocaust rest in an affirmation of a process understanding of God, much less a process theodicy. What those theologians who accept these process categories (for example, God as "all-powerful" and "all-knowing" means the greatest power and knowledge coherently conceivable not verbalizable) can do, I suggest, is to radicalize the process understanding of God *as love*. Thus would the negativity present in the suffering always/already present in genuine love be deliberately rethought in relationship to God's own reality.

I mentioned earlier that for Christian theology, the Holocaust releases a suspicion upon theology. Here it releases a suspicion upon any easy (and easily sentimentalized) notions of God as a God of love and, through that suspicion, releases as well a recognition of the need for theologians to reconsider the possibility of retrieving often-overlooked resources in three areas: first, in the Hebrew Scriptures (Job, Lamentations 3, Amos, Isaiah); second, in the usually overlooked resources of negative theologies in the later Christian tradition itself (Pseudo-Dionysius, Eckhart, Boehme, Schelling); third, in the often-noted but too seldom employed negative elements in the classical theologies of Augustine, Aquinas, Luther, Calvin, Barth, Rahner. It is these resources, I believe, that most need reflection and, if possible, retrieval in the post-Holocaust reflections of all Christian theologians, whether traditional or process. I cannot pretend to have undertaken that necessary reflection on possibilities of retrieval with anything like adequacy. Yet I can and do suggest that even my own process theological understanding of God must radicalize its own self-understanding of the reality of the negative in God.

For myself that means that we must rethink anew the reality of suffering in the reality of God's own self as the self who is love. I believe, with Dietrich Bonhoeffer, that "only a suffering God can help us now." I believe, with the often-repressed strains of the Scriptures of both traditions, Jewish and Christian, that our God is none other than pure, unbounded love—the God who radically affects and is affected by (that is, suffers) the evil we, not God, persist in inflicting upon God's creation. I believe, therefore, that the unspeakable suffering of the six million is also the voice of the suffering of God. It is for us to hear that cry—the cry at once of our fellow human beings and the cry of God's chosen people become the cry of God. Like all the commands of God, this command to hear that lament and that suffering is a command which can enable and empower all who hear it to real action in real history. For all those who hear that voice—the voice of our suffering, betrayed God (betrayed by us) and the voice of God's suffering, betrayed people (betrayed by us)—that voice can become the bond that unites us all in calling out together, with them and with our God, "Never again!"

Notes

1. See Arthur Cohen, *The Tremendum: A Theological Interpretation of the Holocaust* (New York, 1981).

2. I have defended this interpretation of the nature of systematic theology in *The Analogical Imagination: Christian Theology and the Culture of Pluralism* (New York, 1981).

3. The categories "hermeneutics of retrieval" and "hermeneutics of suspicion" are Paul Ricoeur's; inter alia, see his *Freud and Philosophy* (New Haven, 1970). For my own use of these categories in relation to the event of the Holocaust, see the hermeneutical companion piece to this present article, "History, Historicity and Holocaust," from the Indiana University conference on the Holocaust (forthcoming from Indiana University Press).

4. See Cohen, *The Tremendum*; Emil Fackenheim, *God's Presence in History* (New York, 1970); idem, *The Jewish Return into History* (New York, 1978); Irving Greenberg, his several essays on the covenantal theme in post-Holocaust Jewish thought.

5. See E. P. Sanders, *Paul and Palestinian Judaism: A Comparison of Patterns of Religion* (Philadelphia, 1977).

6. Johann Baptist Metz, *Faith in History and Society: Toward a Practical Fundamental Theology* (New York, 1980).

7. See my *Blessed Rage for Order* (New York, 1975).

Afterword

ALFRED GOTTSCHALK

When I formally opened the symposium "Religion in a Post-Holocaust World," I expressed the feeling that I did so with a sense of awe and reverence. I expressed those emotions because I felt that the assembled audience of Christians and Jews was standing on holy ground. The holy ground was the ground characterized by, but not necessarily totally identified with, Auschwitz. As I listened to the words spoken by Christians and Jews, I felt the attempt to bridge differences, to try to understand each other in terms of theologies and as human beings. And yet, between the cadence of words, I still heard gaps of silence, perhaps not unlike the story told by Rabbi Michael Williams, the rabbi of the synagogue in the Rue Copernic in Paris which was bombed not long ago. When the rabbi expected the compassion and understanding of the citizens and neighbors living near the synagogue at the time it was bombed, he received instead bills for the windows of surrounding apartment houses that were broken by the bomb blast.

We have yet a bit to go in understanding one another. A Hasidic rabbi, responding to a friend who said to him, "But I love you, I love you," replied, "How can you love me? You don't know what hurts me!" We have to spend some time talking not about how we love one another but about what it is that hurts us as Christians and Jews.

In statements made by my Christian colleagues during our symposium, I felt that they still did not understand the real meaning of Israel to the Jewish people. One can understand the theological meaning of Israel and one can understand its political meaning. But more fundamental is to understand the human dimension of the meaning of Israel. For without Israel, the Jewish people lives again as a ghost nation, hostage to every dictator and every oppressor and without a homeland to which to turn. That is the fundamental differential that exists and must be understood if one wishes to understand what it is to be a Jew in the post-Holocaust world and what, I suspect, it means to be a Christian.

This volume, we hope, will be thought of as the beginning of a dialogue between scholars, clergy, and members of the lay community. I am grateful to the seminarians, their professors, and to the hundreds of men and women who came with open minds and open hearts to confront and explore the very difficult questions that marked our symposium. We have yet to find the answers to most of these questions. But the importance, for instance, of a Book of Job does not lie in the last chapter which pastes over the greatness of Job's questions. And perhaps it is appropriate to end this volume with Job's statement "Though he slay me, yet I will trust in him." This, in a sense, is the existential statement of the Jewish people and of all people today who have suffered and who will continue to suffer in this world of imperfections. I am by nature a hopeful person. I think together we can find solutions to the problems of life which inundate us and which test us. And no less than Abraham shall we be tested again and again as to whether or not we as members of the civilized religious community are willing to offer up anyone as a sacrifice, even though it be demanded by God . . . even though it be demanded by God.

Contributors

Allan R. Brockway is Associate for Christian-Jewish Relations, Dialogue with People of Living Faiths and Ideologies (DFI), World Council of Churches, Geneva, Switzerland

John S. Conway is Professor of History at the University of British Columbia

Yaffa Eliach is Director of the Brooklyn Center for Holocaust Studies and Associate Professor of Judaic Studies at Brooklyn College in New York

Alfred Gottschalk is President of the Hebrew Union College-Jewish Institute of Religion in Cincinnati, Ohio

Irving Greenberg is Director of the National Jewish Resource Center in New York and Professor of Jewish History at the City College of New York

Abraham J. Peck is Associate Director of the American Jewish Archives in Cincinnati, Ohio and a lecturer at the University of Cincinnati

Rosemary Radford Ruether is Georgia Harkness Professor at the Garrett-Evangelical Theological Seminary in Evanston, Illinois

David W. Tracy is Professor of Theology at the University of Chicago

Elie Wiesel is Andrew W. Mellon Professor in the Humanities at Boston University and Chairman of the United States Holocaust Memorial Council